"I highly recommend this book for anyone who wants to more fully understand the fundamentals of worship and who is willing to respond to God with greater passion in every dimension of their being. This book will stretch you and remind you what is at the very core of our worship. I want our entire church congregation to read it!"

—NANCY BEACH, teaching pastor at Willow Creek Church,
author of *An Hour on Sunday*

"It is tragic irony that amidst the proliferation and popularity of 'worship music', the people of God have developed such an anemic understanding of worship itself. Bob Rognlien has just the cure. This book, in plain and straightforward language, outlines for every believer just what it means to engage the living Christ in biblical worship. It is bound to serve the church well for years to come."

—GLENN PACKIAM, director of New Life School of Worship,
author of *Butterfly in Brazil*, member of Desperation Band

"Bob Rognlien knows that as we worship, so we believe and so we live. This excellent book moves us deeper than performance and show, lecture and program, to discover a way of worship that is transforming to the worshiper and honoring to God."

—BRIAN D. MCLAREN, pastor,
author of *A New Kind of Christian* and *Everything Must Change,*
www.brianmclaren.net

"As an experiential worshiper (not leader), I'm so excited about this book. I long for every person in America—and beyond—to read it, embrace it, and find a whole new understanding of true worship. I caught a glimpse in my reading of what it can be/should be/could be . . . and now I'll be putting it into action in my ongoing worship life."

—LISA T. BERGREN, best-selling novelist,
author of *The Gifted* trilogy, www.lisatawnbergren.com

"Finally. A book on worship for regular people . . . ordinary folks who desire an extraordinary life with God, both inside and outside the worship center. Bravo!"

—SALLY MORGENTHALER, author of *Worship Evangelism*
www.trueconversations.com

"Bob Rognlien has cooked up an earthy recipe for a healthy worship diet. In a culture that loves to consume, here's a refreshing collection of ingredients that lead to a deeper look at what we taste when we worship."

—HANDT HANSON, worship leader, author of *Mission-Driven Worship,*
composer of "Lord, Make My Heart Good Soil," www.handtworks.com

GIVING YOURSELF
MORE COMPLETELY
TO GOD

THE *Experiential*
WORSHIPER

Bob Rognlien

ISBN 978-0-9815247-0-2

Cover design by Timothy J. Bergren,
www.bergrencreativegroup.com

Interior design by Pat Reinheimer
typemaster@mac.com

Rognlien, Bob, 1964-
    The Experiential Worshiper: Giving Yourself More
Completely to God / Bob Rognlien
        p. cm.
    ISBN 978-0-9815247-0-2
1. Worship. 2. Spirituality. 3. Christianity. I. Title

Printed in the United States of America

To my mom Celeste,
who patiently showed me authentic worship begins
with a heart humbled before God;
and my dad Phil,
who fearlessly modeled for me the freedom
of an undignified worshiper:
I owe so much of who I am to you both,
thank you for your stubborn determination to love me
no matter what!

How can we thank God enough for you
in return for all the joy that we feel before our God because of you?

1 THESSALONIANS 3:9

CONTENTS

ACKNOWLEDGMENTS

Worshiping God is a life-long odyssey which ultimately prepares us for eternity. My journey toward becoming an Experiential Worshiper has been furthered by countless family, friends, and mentors along the way who have loved me, guided me, and welcomed me to the banquet table. This little book is a testimony to their faithfulness and the grace of the God who alone satisfies all our longings.

I want to thank my pair of literary sages, Lisa Bergren and Rachelle Gardner, who inspire me to continue writing and show me the way. Thanks to Dana Hanson, John Rudow, and Greg Wallace who read the manuscript and made it a better book; Pam Rognlien who sniffed out the most persistent errors; Tim Bergren who created a cover that would help readers rightly judge its contents; Pat Reinheimer who designed a beautiful interior; and Jim Murrell who got ink on paper to produce this book.

Special thanks to the leaders of Good Shepherd who graciously afforded me time to write and the members of my staff who contributed to this project in so many ways: Kristen Anwandter, Carla Conte, Lea Emerson, Mark Emerson, Kerrie Goachee, Florence Jarrett, Ellen Paulson, Dave Peters, Lisa Such,

Gloria Sugden, Cindi Wallace, and Greg Wallace. Thanks to the members of my small group, my writer-pastors group, my colleague-pastors group, and the countless prayer warriors who carry me through every day.

Above all, I want to thank the members of my family who bring me untold joy: Mom for unconditional love, Dad for unconditional faith, Leslie for a friendship stronger than blood, Bobby for making me laugh, Luke for making me smile, and Pamela for being the great love of my life. I am so blessed to be seated around the table with each one of you!

Chapter 1

COME JOIN THE FEAST!

A BANQUET FIT FOR A KING

I can never decide which inspires greater delight: the sight of a dining table fit for a medieval king or the mouthwatering smells pouring out of my mother's tiny kitchen. Ever since our boys were young it has been a tradition for us to spend Thanksgiving with my mom at her third story Victorian flat on Russian Hill in San Francisco. With countless shelves of leather-bound books, carved antique furniture, and sweeping views of the Bay, it is a place so unlike our own suburban tract home that it evokes a sense of wonder in all four of us. Bobby and Luke bound up the long flight of worn stairs excitedly announcing our arrival, followed by my wife, Pam, bearing our culinary contribution to the feast. I typically bring up the rear, lugging bags like some kind of stamina-challenged Sherpa.

My mom loves to go all out for her family. Preparations begin weeks ahead of time: ordering the fresh (never frozen) turkey of unnatural proportions; gathering ingredients for all our favorite family recipes; unpacking heirloom china and crystal; ironing the Italian lace tablecloth; polishing silver tableware and serving dishes. An overhead spotlight illuminates the specially-designed seasonal centerpiece, complete with fresh-cut flowers and candles. Each place is set with three china plates, crystal goblets of varying dimensions, an embroidered linen napkin, and silverware for every conceivable category of food.

Cooking begins days ahead of time with a flurry of chopping, dicing, slicing, and baking. Famous family recipes are consulted like trustworthy sages. The gigantic proportions of each dish matches the alarming size of a bird obviously never meant to fly. The turkey is stuffed, sewn, tied, rubbed, basted, and squeezed into a hot oven. Finally a procession of serving dishes bear this extravagant bounty to the table, filling every available space and overflowing onto a serving table: roast turkey, homemade stuffing, rich gravy, riced potatoes, my sister Leslie's scalloped corn, my brother Joe's sweet potatoes, my grandma Mukkie's Norwegian lefse and kringle, butternut squash, buttery rolls, cranberry sauce, cranberry jelly, cranberry relish, cranberry everything! Then comes the triumphal moment when we all sit down to a feast exceeding the dreams of even the greediest pilgrim.

There are few experiences I enjoy more than a delicious meal shared with people I love. Sitting around my mother's table, holding hands in prayer, my soul swells with a feeling of gratitude and love for the people so deeply connected to my life. Savoring each bite, my whole body responds with appreciation. Amidst the mmm's, the laughter, and the conversation, my mind fills with memories of Thanksgivings gone by and a greater understanding of just how blessed I really am. Deep in my heart there wells up a stronger resolve never to take these blessings for granted and to give back to others out of all that

I have so graciously received. Sitting at that family feast is like tasting a slice of heaven!

Don't you wish it was possible to seal moments like that in a jar so you could savor them again when loneliness gnaws at your soul? But of course we can't; those moments slip through our fingers only to be recalled as distant memories. The hunger remains. The loneliness creeps in. Deep inside we know we were made for something different, that somewhere, there is a table with a place set for us. A place where we belong, where our deepest hungers inside are finally fed.

THE HEAVENLY BANQUET

Reading the Gospels I get the sense that Jesus relished a good meal with loved ones even more than I. From the wedding party of Cana to the banquet table of Simon the Pharisee, we often hear about Jesus enjoying fancy dinners with friends and strangers alike. He was so eager to share a table with people of every walk of life that it confounded the sensibilities of religious people like the Pharisees who asked him with annoyance, "Why do you eat and drink with tax collectors and sinners?" (Luke 5:30). Others criticized Jesus directly for this perceived excess, labeling him "a glutton and a drunkard" (Luke 7:34). So it comes as no surprise that Jesus likened the kingdom of God to "a king who gave a wedding banquet for his son" (Matthew 22:2). So much for clouds and harps! In these verses, we see that a far more biblical image for heaven is the image of an eternal feast hosted by our heavenly Father where we will enjoy each other's company forever!

To point us toward our ultimate destiny God gave the prophet Isaiah a glimpse of this heavenly banquet: "On this mountain the LORD of hosts will make for all peoples a feast of rich food, a feast of well-aged wines, of rich food filled with marrow, of well-aged wines strained clear" (Isaiah 25:6). It makes my mouth water right now just picturing it! Clearly Isaiah is talking about more than just food here, but don't you find yourself wondering what it is about heaven that will fill us with joy like "a feast of rich food" and "well-aged wines"?

Centuries later the Apostle John was given an unprecedented peek into heaven itself. He saw God seated on the throne with the Lamb that was slain, surrounded by twenty-four elders, four living creatures, myriads of angels, and ultimately every creature in creation (Revelation 4-5). Do you know what they were doing? They were falling on their faces before the throne and the Lamb, casting down their golden crowns, giving God glory, honor, thanks, and blessing; recognizing his power, wealth, and wisdom. Among other choruses, a continual song rose day and night around this throne: "Holy, holy, holy, the Lord God the Almighty, who was and is and is to come" (Revelation 4:8). All the creatures of creation were experiencing the complete holiness and wonder of God's very nature and it was evoking in them an unrestrained offering of their whole selves to God in ceaseless worship!

COME TASTE AND SEE

Worship is the eternal activity of heaven. God himself is the main course of the eternal heavenly banquet. Isaiah's prophecy describes nothing less than a complete experience of God in which we give all we are back to him in worship. The psalmist invites us to "taste and see that the LORD is good" (Psalm 34:8). No wonder Jesus left us with a meal in which he offers us his "body" and "blood" (Matthew 26:26-28). He knew the root of every longing in the human heart is a hunger for God. The gnawing in our souls, the cold edge of loneliness, the constant desire for something *more* is in actuality our innate desire to be deeply connected to God.

From the beginning we were created for intimate relationship with our Creator. Absolute fulfillment in Eden sprang from the perfect union between God and his children. The tragedy of sin is that it separates us from God and robs us of that union for which we were created. That great leader of the ancient church, Augustine of Hippo, who embraced Christ after a long season of rebellion, came to realize his desire for the things of this world was ultimately driven by a hunger for God. He describes his realization in this poetic prayer:

Late have I loved you, O beauty so ancient and new. Late have I loved you!
You were within me while I have gone outside to seek you. Unlovely
myself, I rushed toward all those lovely things you had made. And
always you were with me, and I was not with you.
All these beauties kept me far from you—although they would not have
existed at all unless they had their being in you.
    You called,
        you cried,
            you shattered my deafness.
    You sparkled,
        you blazed,
            you drove away my blindness.
You shed your fragrance, I drew in my breath, and I pant for you. I tasted
and now I hunger and thirst. You touched me, and now I burn with
longing for your peace.[1]

When finally we experience the purity and holiness of God everything else pales by comparison. As we begin to taste the fullness of God and give ourselves back to him in self-abandonment it awakens a longing, a burning in our hearts, a hunger gnawing in our souls, driving us deeper into the mystery and wonder of worshiping God with all that we are. The perfect wholeness of Jesus' kingdom will be realized as every creature recognizes God for who he really is and honors him as such.

> "The divine paradox of the heavenly feast is that we will be most satisfied the more completely we give ourselves away to God and others."

The divine paradox of the heavenly feast is that we will be most satisfied the more completely we give ourselves away to God and others. This paradoxical truth is what Jesus pointed us to when he said, "For those who want to save their life will lose it, and those who lose their life for my sake will find it" (Matthew 16:25).

Are you tired of nibbling on memories sealed in a jar? Is there a gnawing loneliness in your soul telling you there must be something more? Like the young Augustine have you been rushing toward those "lovely things" around you rather than the One who made them lovely? Have you been going outside yourself to seek the One who is already within you? Don't make the mistake he made and allow the beauties of this world to keep you far from God any longer. You don't want to look back one day and say with regret as he did, "Late have I loved you, O beauty so ancient and new!"

Genuine worship gives us a foretaste of the restored Eden yet to come and leads us on the path toward recovering who we really are and why we are here. There is a place set for you, a place you belong, where the gnawing in your soul can finally be satisfied. I invite you — no, I challenge you — to come to the table and join the feast. Come and taste the kind of worship that calls you to give all you are; the kind of worship that will leave you panting and burning with an ever-greater longing for more of God!

FOR REFLECTION AND DISCUSSION

1. What is one of the best meals you can remember? What made it so great?

2. What are you hungry for in your life? What are some ways you try to satiate that hunger?

3. Can you relate to Jesus' image of heaven as a banquet? Why or why not?

4. In what way is worship like partaking in that banquet?

5. Read Revelation 4:1-11. When you imagine John's description of heaven, how does it make you feel? What kind of longings does it awaken in you?

Chapter 2

MISSING INGREDIENTS?

PANCAKES, FRISBEES, OR HOCKEY PUCKS?

I have always been a pancake lover. Nothing quite compares to the smell of a buttermilk pancake sizzling on a hot griddle. I can trace it back to my grandfather, who we called "Bompa." Every summer he would host a large breakfast at the family cabin on Flathead Lake in Montana, cooking hotcakes on a huge cast iron griddle over an open fire. Though Bompa received all the accolades, my grandmother Myrna actually made the batter and did most of the work. Once, when he ran out of batter and called for Myrna in the kitchen to make more, his cover was broken. As one scandalized friend exclaimed, "If Myrna makes the batter, what are *you* good for? Any *baboon* can flip 'em!"

When I was twenty-four, about four years after my grandfather's death, I reinstituted the tradition, establishing the annual "Baboon Memorial Pancake Breakfast" in honor of both Bompa and Myrna. Cooking over the same wood-fired griddle every summer, I make it a point to make the batter *and* flip 'em. I have to admit that over the years I have become a bit of a batter snob. The very thought of packaged pancake mix sends a shiver up my spine—only fresh buttermilk batter made from scratch will ever touch my griddle!

But I have learned the hard way that one missing ingredient can ruin those fluffy pancakes. It doesn't matter how fresh the buttermilk is or how light you whip the eggs, if you forget the baking power, you are in for serious trouble. There is nothing worse than watching children use your hotcakes as Frisbees or hockey pucks! It's amazing the radical effect a single missing ingredient can have on what otherwise would have been a delicious meal.

How Does Your Worship Taste?

While you were reading about worship as a heavenly feast did you get a bad taste in your mouth? Did you find yourself wondering why your experience of worship does not feel like sitting down at a banquet table where new passions are ignited and old longings satisfied? Have you been attending worship services hoping to bite into a fluffy pancake, only to discover a hockey puck between your teeth? Maybe you are one of those people who goes to church every week hoping for some comfort, strength, peace, hope, joy, inspiration, or guidance, only to walk away empty and disappointed. Or maybe you don't even have high enough expectations to be disappointed, but you wonder if gathering with others to worship is really worth your time and effort.

And unfortunately, it's easy to assign blame: "The pastor just doesn't inspire me." "The sermons are boring and predictable." "The worship leader is not very talented." "The music is not my style." "The service is too traditional." "The service is too contemporary." "It's too long." "It's not long enough." "It's too structured." "It has no structure." "It's out of date." "It's too trendy." "It's too early." "It's too late." We point our finger at anything and everything but ourselves. Some of us stubbornly hang in there and slowly become discouraged or jaded. Some of us move on to another church but the dissatisfaction stays the same. Only the excuses change. Some of us quietly slip into inactivity and focus on other, "more important" things.

Wherever we find ourselves, all of us sense deep inside there must be more to the worship experience than hockey pucks or Frisbees. We sense it because our heart and soul longs for the fluffy pancake that melts in the mouth, the perfect food that lands satisfyingly in our stomachs. Maybe that's what has kept you hanging in there and coming back—the hope for just the right recipe, just around the corner, the time when it all perfectly comes together. Maybe that's what caused you to pick up this book and read this far, so you could hand it to your pastor and say, "Here! This is the way!"

But the answer does not lie in better preaching, more relevant music, or a service redesigned to meet your tastes, helpful as those might be. The answer lies with us, with the worshiper. Ultimately we are the ones who determine the quality of our worship experience, because *worship is our response to God's love.* God initiates worship, graciously coming to us, but in the end, responsibility for our response falls to each one of us.

> "Ultimately we are the ones who determine the quality of our worship experience, because *worship is our response to God's love.*"

In her book *The Cloister Walk,* Kathleen Norris describes how she learned this lesson after spending time as a Protestant

Christian living in Catholic monasteries. "Even when I find church boring I hold this in mind as a possibility: like all the other fools who have dragged themselves to church on Sunday morning, including the pastor, I am there because I need to be reminded that love can be at the center of all things, if we will only keep it there. The worship service will most likely not offer an aesthetically pleasing experience, great theological insight, or emotional release, although any and all of those things are possible, and precious."[2]

This observation is a stinging indictment of our public worship gatherings. It is sad that most services in and of themselves do not more fully move people. This realization should motivate those of us who plan and lead to do all we can to design services that help people experience God more completely.[3] However, at the same time Norris helps us understand the key to fulfillment as a worshiper is learning to love God with all we are, regardless of the shape or style of our worship environment.

Too often we want to point the finger of blame at others for what is lacking in our worship experience. Paul says, "Why do you pass judgment on your brother or sister? Or you, why do you despise your brother or sister? For we will all stand before the judgment seat of God. For it is written, 'As I live, says the Lord, every knee shall bow to me, and every tongue shall give praise to God.' So then, each of us will be accountable to God" (Romans 14:10-12). If our worship is lacking something, if we have a bad taste in our mouth, most likely the problem lies with us. Maybe it is because we have been using the wrong recipe in our personal approach to worship. Perhaps we have not yet learned how to bring all the right ingredients to Jesus' banquet table.

What Recipe Are You Using?

Some of us have been taught the key to worship is just *showing up.* If we are filling a seat, then we are worshiping. According to this worship recipe the question is not "Did we worship?" but "Did we go to church?" The focus is on attendance. Attention is given to appearance. Importance is attached to what others think of us. Worship is reduced to outward ritual regardless of its inward meaning. Attending public worship gatherings becomes something to check off our "To Do" list. We get credit for being there. We get it done so we can move on to other, more important things in our day.

Others of us assume worship is *a spectator sport.* We buy our ticket, we sit in the stands, and we watch the professionals do it—supposedly better than we ever could. In this recipe worship is passive. We watch. We listen. There is no perceived need to participate. Worship is judged by how well others performed. We silently score the sermon, the music, the readers, the sound system, the lights, the décor, the loud guy singing off-key behind us. And then we leave, tabulating how they all did, secretly relieved we don't have to step forward and be scored ourselves.

But the most common worship recipe today is *the consumer mindset.* We ask, "What do I like? What do I want? How does it make me feel? Is it convenient? Is it comfortable? Does it fit into my lifestyle? Does it meet my needs?" Worship is judged by how effectively it fulfills our personal expectations. With this approach, worshipers are the customers and the worship leaders are the service providers. People enter church much the same way they might enter Wal-Mart or Costco, expecting their needs to be met in the most efficient way possible at the lowest price they can find. We come to church hoping to get a lot of "bang for our buck!"

A Biblical Recipe

The Bible offers us a radically different kind of worship recipe. We discover worship is not primarily about us. The focus of biblical worship is always God. Genuine worship leads us from the prison of self-absorption to the freedom of self-abandonment. Worship is not a spectator sport, it is about full participation. We are the players, not the fans, and our leaders are the player-coaches, not the star performers. And worship is about far more than attendance. It is made up of outward actions that flow from inward realities. It forms a lifestyle of integrity in which we are continually giving ourselves back to God in all that we do.

If going to church has left a bad taste in our mouth—or left us still hungering for the worship banquet—maybe it's time to reconsider how we approach it. Maybe it's time to recover biblical ingredients of worship we might be missing. Maybe it's time to ask Jesus about his recipe for worship.

For Reflection and Discussion

1. What kind of taste does your current experience of worship leave in your mouth—more like fluffy pancakes or hockey pucks?

2. What are some of the complaints you have had about the worship gatherings you attend?

3. Who do you think is ultimately responsible for the quality of your worship life? Explain.

4. How would you describe your "recipe" for worship: showing up, spectator, consumer, or something else?

5. Read Romans 14:10-12. Why are we so quick to judge others and so slow to hold ourselves accountable? How can you apply Paul's admonition to your worship life?

Chapter 3

Jesus' Recipe for Worship

What Really Matters?

Elias had heard the rumors of his power and authority for months, but until he saw this Jesus of Nazareth with his own eyes, he dismissed them all as idle tales. Talk of wonder-workers and would-be Messiahs was rampant in these days of unrest, especially in Jerusalem during the Passover feast. And now the infamous Galilean rabbi and his motley band of so-called disciples had come into the city and were causing all kinds of commotion, especially at the temple. Elias heard Jesus had actually knocked over the tables of the money changers and driven out those selling animals for sacrifice. As a scribe and an educated student of the Torah, Elias resented the crass use of the holy precincts for commerce, but this was going too far! Obviously this Jesus was an unstable and dangerous man.

The next morning Elias woke with a start. He had no business at the temple that day, but something drew him anyway. As he hurried up the grand staircase to the massive temple courts, his heartbeat quickened in anticipation. There in Solomon's Portico underneath the gigantic limestone columns, a crowd had gathered around Jesus and some Pharisees.

Elias edged closer to hear.

The rabbi was telling a parable when a prominent Pharisee, together with a member of Herod's court, stepped forward to ask him a trick question. Jesus' answer somehow put *them* on the spot instead of him. Then two members of the Sadducees asked Jesus another question, but again, without missing a beat, Jesus answered in a way that amazed even those who were trying to trap him.

By this time Elias had made his way to the front of the crowd. Maybe it was his role as a scribe that caused others to show deference, or maybe it was the magnetic pull he felt from this strange and surprising rabbi, but whatever the reason suddenly Elias found himself standing before Jesus.

Through the years Elias had grown tired of all the wrangling among his colleagues over the minutiae of the Law while ignoring the spirit of the Law. Increasingly, Elias found himself searching for the key that would take him beyond the rules of right and wrong into a life of meaning and purpose.

As Elias studied the face of this man who stood before him he realized Jesus was different. Perhaps someone who could stump Pharisees, snare Sadducees, and evoke such outlandish rumors could offer insight into the real meaning of the Law. Before he remembered to be intimidated, Elias blurted out his question, "Which commandment is the first of all?"

Jesus looked deep into his eyes and answered, "The first is, 'Hear, O Israel: the Lord our God, the Lord is one; you shall love the Lord your God with all your heart, and with all your soul, and with all your mind, and with all your strength.' The second is this, 'You shall love your neighbor as yourself.' There is no other commandment greater than these."

Something stirred within Elias. A voice inside him cried "Yes!" For the rest of his life Jesus' words were burned into Elias's memory: "love the Lord your God with all your heart, and with all your soul, and with all your mind, and with all your strength . . . love your neighbor as yourself." (Based on Mark 12:1-34)

THE GREAT WORSHIP COMMANDMENT

Love God with all we are and love our neighbor as ourselves—amazingly Jesus captures everything that matters in life with a phrase so simple a child can grasp it! And yet the more we reflect on this profound statement, the more we are challenged to consider its full implications. What does it really mean to "love God"? It's easier to imagine how to apply the second commandment because our "neighbor" is a tangible reality we can see, touch, and love in concrete actions. But what about God? How do you love the invisible, ineffable, almighty Creator of the universe? At least the disciples had the historical Jesus—the fishermen could answer his call to leave their nets, Mary could wipe his feet with her hair, Peter could step out of his boat and follow him onto the water. But how are we to love the God we cannot touch or see? Jesus said loving "one of the least of these" was a way of loving God (Matthew 25:40), but that brings us back to the second commandment again.

To love God with all our heart, soul, mind, and strength can be expressed in anything we do that serves Jesus Christ and the Kingdom of God. This encompasses all of our lives, from the simple and ordinary to the extravagant and sublime. We are all called to love God indirectly by the way we live

"The beauty and wonder of worship lies in the fact it is the only thing we can give to God that he does not already have."

our lives every day. *However, there is one way we can express our love to God directly and specifically: worship.* The beauty and wonder of worship lies in the fact it is the only thing we can give to God that he does not already have. Worship is the one thing we do exclusively to express our love to God.

If the great commandment applies to our worship, it means there is nothing more important than worshiping God in a way that leads us to love others as well. Jesus is giving us his recipe for worship the way it is meant to be. What does it mean to worship God with our heart, soul, mind, and strength? A closer look at these four biblical terms will help us better understand Jesus' vision for true worship.

HeartWorship

In our culture the heart is a symbol for strong, positive emotions. One glimpse at a card shop in February is enough to prove this point. Try to find a Valentine's Day card without a heart on it! Not so in biblical times. In the Bible the word "heart" points to *human will*, that amazing and terrifying power of choice God gave when he created us. We can see this when the Psalmist writes, "Happy are those who keep his decrees, who seek him with their whole heart" (Psalm 119:2). Paul demonstrates this understanding of the word when he admonishes Christian slaves to do "the will of God from the heart" (Ephesians 6:6). The biblical authors understood "heart" as the place where human intention resides.

To love God with all our heart is to choose worship as a

response to God's grace. This worship is not based on feelings or circumstances, but on a decision to respond to the amazing grace and love of God in Jesus. "HeartWorship" is responding to God on the *volitional* level of human experience. This is not to say we exercise our will independently of God's Spirit. Ultimately all right decisions and good choices are empowered by the gracious presence of God within us. But God's Spirit is never coercive. Our will is critical because, like love, in order for worship to be genuine it must be freely chosen. *When you make a deliberate choice to thank, honor, or glorify God, receive forgiveness, listen to his Word, or submit to God's will, you are worshiping God with your heart.*

SoulWorship

Most people in our society today, including many Christians, use the term "soul" to describe a ghost-like reality that makes up the immortal identity of individuals and survives physical death. However, this is really an ancient Greek concept of the soul and is found nowhere in the Bible. The biblical writers use the term "soul" in various ways, but primarily to describe *the way we feel* and our expression of those feelings. We can see this when the Psalmists exclaim, "Then my soul shall rejoice in the LORD, exulting in his deliverance" and "Why are you cast down, O my soul, and why are you disquieted within me?" (Psalm 35:9; 42:11). The same idea is reflected in our use of the term "psychological," which is based on the Greek word for the soul, *psuche.* The biblical writers use the term "soul" to describe the seat of our emotions.

To love God with all our soul is to pour out our feelings to God as an act of worship. "SoulWorship" is responding to God on the *emotional* level of human experience. *When you feel the joy of your salvation, sorrow for your sin, or hope in the plans God has for you and then offer these emotions to God, you are worshiping with your soul.* This does not mean worship is based on feelings, because they come and go like the wind. It does mean our response in worship includes emotional passion as a crucial part of offering ourselves to God.

MindWorship

We tend to think of the mind as a computer, an organ that stores, processes, and retrieves information. However, the biblical writers use the term "mind" to describe not just our ability to process information, but a consciousness enabling us to *derive meaning and wisdom* from that information. This biblical view of the mind emphasizes "knowing," which is both fact-based and relational. When Solomon asks for wisdom God responds, "I give you a wise and discerning mind" (1 Kings 3:12). Paul describes Christian unity as being of "one mind" (Philippians 2:2) and Christian maturity as gaining "the mind of Christ" (1 Corinthians 2:16). The biblical writers see the mind as a network connecting the various aspects of human experience and leading us toward deeper meaning.

To love God with all our mind is to use our intellect to engage God's revealed truth and respond with meaning-full expressions of worship. In thought-full worship our full attention is focused on the God we are glorifying. There is no such thing as mindless worship, because such an expression is literally meaningless. MindWorship is responding to God on the cognitive level of human experience. *When you focus your thoughts on God, seek to understand God's Word, grapple with insights that go beyond simple logic, reflect on the words you are singing or praying, and compose meaningful expressions of awe and wonder, you are worshiping God with your mind.*

Strength Worship

Many people assume "spirituality" is somehow the opposite of "physicality." This is a profoundly unbiblical view. From the first moment of creation in Genesis to the final apocalyptic re-creation in Revelation, the Bible offers an unwavering affirmation of the goodness of the physical order and its direct connection to spiritual realities. That God took on a physical identity in Jesus is central to our faith. Any truly biblical view of worship will take the same inclusive view of the human body.

In the Scriptures, "strength" sometimes refers to personal determination, other times to moral conviction, but it is often connected to the *physical* aspect of human existence. Proverbs 20:29 uses this word to describe the aging process of the body: "The glory of youths is their strength, but the beauty of the aged is their gray hair." Sometimes lack of physical strength is described: "My strength fails because of my misery, and my bones waste away" (Psalm 31:10). Even when physical strength is used as a spiritual metaphor, physical images are used: "But those who wait for the LORD shall renew their strength, they shall mount up with wings like eagles, they shall run and not be weary, they shall walk and not faint" (Isaiah 40:31).

When Jesus calls us to love God with all we are, he not only includes our will, our emotions, and our intellect, but he puts all these aspects of our humanity in the context of our physical being. To love God with our strength means to allow our bodies to give expression to the thoughts, feelings, and decisions that reflect the response of the whole person to God. This is worship expressed through more than just the vocal cords. This is worship that engages every part of our physical being, all our senses. This is worship that utilizes our body as an instrument of praise to glorify God. This is worship that leads us to do God's will in our daily lives and so bring honor to him. "StrengthWorship" is responding to God with your whole body. *When you bow in humility, kneel in confession, stand in awe, clap in celebration, cross yourself in reverence, lift your hands in praise, dance for joy, or reach out a hand to someone in need, you are worshiping God with all of your strength.*

THE FOUR KEY INGREDIENTS

When Jesus answered that well-meaning scribe with the greatest of all commandments, he was outlining for us the four key ingredients of biblical worship and how we are meant to encounter God:

HUMAN EXPERIENCE IN WORSHIP

BIBLICAL TERM	HUMAN TRAIT	RESPONSE IN WORSHIP
Heart	Volitional	What we choose
Soul	Emotional	What we feel
Mind	Intellectual	What we think
Strength	Physical	What we do

When all four of these aspects of human experience come together in worship we encounter God in such a way that we are moved to give our whole selves back to him. This is the worship Jesus calls us to in his great commandment.

COMPARING RECIPES

I once had the opportunity to live and study in Jerusalem for an entire school year. It was an amazing experience for many reasons, one of which was the exposure to so many different forms of worship. That year, during the Week of Prayer for Christian Unity, the various churches in Jerusalem organized a week-long series of ecumenical services to be held in a different kind of church each evening. I attended all of them and my eyes were opened to the incredible diversity of worship forms that comprise our faith. Some services were more formal and helped me to experience the mysterious transcendence of God. Others were more personal and drew me into the intimate presence of God. Some were highly visual in nature, the worship space covered in vivid icons. Others were thoroughly musical, inviting people to sing and outwardly express their love for God.

I was most amazed by the Ethiopian Orthodox service. The intricately decorated sanctuary was a round domed building covered with colorful icons. A small house-shaped structure with open windows and doorways on all four sides stood at the very center under the dome, completely enclosing the altar. The congregation stood all the way around the perimeter of the worship space as the priests went in and out of all four doorways accessing the altar, swinging incense holders and singing the liturgy. Most surprising to me was that not only did they sing the entire liturgy, but the scripture readings and the sermon as well! As odd as this might seem to American Protestant Christians, this is the form of worship that is familiar to Ethiopian Orthodox Christians. I'm sure that a worship service with electric guitars, a video projector, a children's sermon, or an announcement time would seem even stranger to them!

That week of diverse worship gatherings opened my eyes to see that, for all the varied forms of Christian worship, the goal is always the same: facilitating an experience that helps us give ourselves to God in such a way that God is glorified and we are changed. But this variety of worship forms also opened my eyes to see many of us are missing crucial ingredients in Jesus' special recipe for complete worship. The problem is these missing ingredients are keeping us from experiencing God fully and therefore more completely loving God. It is critical to recognize the way each of us approaches worship has been profoundly shaped by the particular traditions and forms of worship to which we have been exposed.

If you grew up in a church with long, in-depth sermons, you may tend toward loving God with your mind. If you worship in a church in which you are regularly called to make strong commitments and where the services often end with an altar call, you may lean toward loving God with your heart. If your weekly worship typically includes kneeling and receiving communion, you may be comfortable loving God with your physical strength. If in your church services people are encouraged to express themselves by laughing, crying, cheering, or even collapsing, then you may be used to loving God with your soul. But what are the ingredients that might be missing from your worship experience?

FOLLOWING JESUS' WORSHIP RECIPE

The secret to a more complete experience of God is bringing together all four of the key ingredients in Jesus' great recipe. I have come to believe most of us are missing out on much of the feast God has for us because we have overlooked crucial ingredients in our worship life. Maybe it is because we have only been exposed to a certain tradition of worship and we simply don't know about the other ingredients. Maybe it is because we have become used to our familiar forms of worship and don't want to be stretched beyond our comfort zones. Or maybe we feel the need to defend our partial recipe by claiming, "This is the way worship is supposed to be!"

Jesus told a story in which someone prepared a great dinner and invited many people, but they each gave lame excuses why they could not attend. Tragically, these invited guests missed out on the greatest party their town had ever seen and the host ended up bringing in anyone who was willing to come (Luke 14:18-20).

You and I are invited to the greatest party of all time. When we are willing to move beyond lame excuses and begin to intentionally love God with all our heart, soul, mind, and strength, the result is a more complete experience of God, which in turn inspires a more complete offering of ourselves to God in worship.

> "When we are willing to move beyond lame excuses and begin to intentionally love God with all our heart, soul, mind, and strength, the result is a more complete experience of God, which in turn inspires a more complete offering of ourselves to God in worship."

There are growing numbers of people today who are no longer satisfied with partial experiences of God. These

"Experiential Worshipers" are hungry for more of God and for a more complete response to him. They are moving beyond familiar patterns and are open to exploring forgotten or ignored ingredients from Jesus' great commandment in their worship life. As they encounter God with their thoughts, emotions, actions, and choices, they discover within a growing passion to love God with all that they are and to love their neighbors as themselves. If you sense this same hunger growing inside of you, if you want to give yourself more fully to God, then I invite you to read on as we explore together what it means to take our place at the great banquet table with Jesus and his people in the feast of Experiential Worship!

FOR REFLECTION AND DISCUSSION

1. Do you think Jesus' great commandment should be applied to our worship life? Why or why not?

2. What does it actually mean for you to "love God"?

3. Which of the four ingredients in Jesus' worship recipe comes the most naturally to you: HeartWorship (will), SoulWorship (emotion), MindWorship (thoughts), or StrengthWorship (physical)?

4. Which of these key ingredients do you think has been lacking in your worship recipe?

5. Read Mark 12:28-34. Why do you think Jesus connects loving God and loving our neighbor? What does that mean for our worship life?

Chapter 4

EXPLORING EXPERIENTIAL WORSHIP

A TEMPLE EXPERIENCE

Anxiety was running rampant in Jerusalem. With King Uzziah dead, over fifty years of stability in Judah had come to an end and many wondered if the new king, Jotham, would be able to handle the pressures his father had managed so well. Shaky political alliances with Israel to the north were made even more tenuous by the fact that the king of Assyria was on the march, moving his unstoppable forces westward. Perhaps it was to be expected during a time as tumultuous as this that Isaiah's vision would take him to the temple in Jerusalem, the heart and soul of the people of Israel. But nothing could have prepared him for what he experienced there.

Isaiah opened spiritual eyes to see something that could not, should not be seen: the Lord himself seated on his throne! This image was too huge to be framed by any earthly reference point, but the bottom edge of the divine robe overflowed the massive temple. Such a king could not be without attendants: flying above him were strange six-winged seraphs, creatures defying description, announcing the identity and character of this enthroned Lord: "Holy, holy, holy is the LORD of hosts;

the whole earth is full of his glory." This pronouncement was so powerful it shook the deep rock foundations of the temple and filled it with smoke.

In despair Isaiah understood the implication of this vision; he was to die, for no sinner can see the true holiness of God and live. "Woe is me! I am lost, for I am a man of unclean lips, and I live among a people of unclean lips; yet my eyes have seen the King, the LORD of hosts!" The prophet's despair melted into terror as one of the seraphs flew toward him, apparently to execute this sentence. But rather than the piercing pain of judgment, he felt instead the cleansing glow of redemption fill his entire body as the creature touched an altar coal to his unclean lips. The seraph spoke the words Isaiah had only dared to hope were true, "Now that this has touched your lips, your guilt has departed and your sin is blotted out."

Relief, mixed with gratitude and unbounded joy, flooded his mind. A sense of freedom and cleansing surged through him as the weight of guilt and shame were lifted from his soul. Then Isaiah heard a voice that cut through every defense and captured his very heart, "Whom shall I send, and who will go for us?" With the glow of redemption still coursing through his veins and the words of atonement ringing in his ears, there was no time for excuses, questions, or conditions. Stepping out in faith, Isaiah made a decision that would forever change his life. He responded, "Here am I; send me!" (Based on Isaiah 6:1-8)

A Worship Experience Unpacked

In the Bible, worship is always a transforming encounter with the living God who engages the whole person. Isaiah's experience at the temple was no less. Notice how seeing God enthroned in power affected him. First, his body was engaged through the senses: he saw the Lord, heard the seraphs, felt the shaking, smelled the smoke, and felt the coal touch his lips. This is StrengthWorship. Second, his mind was engaged. He understood God's holiness was incompatible with his own brokenness. He realized what an amazing gift he was being given in forgiveness. He recognized God's call as an invitation to give himself completely. This is MindWorship. Third, along with these ideas came powerful emotions. He felt awe at the power and holiness of God. He felt shame over his own sin. He felt gratitude for the grace shown to him. This is SoulWorship. Finally, God engaged his will by inviting him to answer a call. He was given a clear invitation and deliberately chose to respond in the power of the Spirit. This is HeartWorship.

In this encounter at the temple, profound truths and vivid images combined with powerful emotions causing the young Isaiah not only to understand God's call, but to respond with conviction and commitment. Our encounters with God may not be so dramatic, but when we experience God on any level physically, intellectually, and emotionally, we are moved to make better choices. This is complete biblical worship involving the heart, mind, soul, and strength. This is what it means to be an Experiential Worshiper.

We can see this same pattern throughout the scriptures: Jacob wrestling with God at Peniel, Moses taking off sandals at the burning bush, the boy Samuel saying "Speak Lord" in the temple, the disciples abandoning their fishing boats, the Samaritan woman offering water at the well, the woman wiping Jesus' feet, Thomas saying "My Lord and my God," the Apostles filled with the Spirit on the day of Pentecost. Why were these such transforming moments in the lives of the people who experienced them? Because in each of these diverse circumstances they opened themselves to God on all four of these levels and responded in kind. If we want to take our place at the banquet table, if we have a growing hunger for more of God, if we want to recapture the power of true biblical worship, we will open ourselves to a more complete experience of God and respond by loving him with all our heart, soul, mind, and strength.

> ". . . if we want to recapture the power of true biblical worship, we will open ourselves to a more complete experience of God and respond by loving him with all our heart, soul, mind, and strength."

WHAT IS WORSHIP?

Before we can explore more fully what it means to worship God with our thoughts, emotions, actions, and choices, we need to clarify what we actually mean by the word "worship." People often use the term to refer to things like singing, programs, liturgies, and musical styles. However, these are just the outward forms that are meant to lead us to worship, they are not worship itself. *Biblical worship is the internal, transforming encounter that these kinds of outward forms can facilitate.*

Sometimes people divide the weekly gathering of God's people into two distinct categories: "worship" and "preaching." In this model worship is primarily seen as singing to God, as opposed to listening to his Word. This distinction misses the point that worship, as an encounter with God, is a two-way street. In biblical worship God comes to us through the Word in the power of the Spirit and offers us love, truth, conviction, grace, forgiveness, comfort, exhortation, and guidance. In humility, gratitude, and faith we respond with things like confession, repentance, commitment, adoration, thanksgiving, intercession, and celebration. The intersection of these two dynamics—God reaching out to us and us responding to him—is what real worship is all about.

Worship leader and songwriter Matt Redman describes worship simply as "revelation and response."[4] I thought this was a new, cutting edge way to describe worship until I read Martin Luther's similar description written 500 years earlier: "[In worship] our dear Lord speaks to us through his holy Word, and we respond to him through our prayer and praise."[5] In the end it is that simple. God comes to us and we respond to him. This encounter is true worship.

A BI-DIRECTIONAL ENCOUNTER WITH GOD

This kind of worship moves us far beyond the singing we do on Sunday morning, into a holistic encounter with God that engages all aspects of human experience. Thus, we begin to see that real worship, loving God, encompasses *everything* that happens in our weekly gatherings, engages us at every level of our experience, and calls us to offer all that we are back to him.

DISTINGUISHING FORM FROM CONTENT

One of the difficulties in defining worship is that we often confuse the outward forms of worship with the actual content of worship. It is critical that we learn to make a clear distinction between these two aspects of public worship. Our heritage, personality, learning styles, tastes, and experiences all contribute to the form or style of worship we prefer. When we experience God we can become attached to the particular style or format that facilitated that experience. We may express these deep attachments in value judgments like "I believe worship should be . . ." or "True worship is always . . ." Rather than describing biblical principles or spiritually substantive aspects of worship, we often point to the form in which these defining encounters with God took place, such as a particular style of music or order of worship. Instead of holding onto the transforming *content* of these worship experiences we often cherish the *form* in which they came to us. The result is a subtle kind of idolatry in which we focus on outward expressions of worship rather than on God, who is the substance of all transforming worship.

When Jesus was talking to the Samaritan woman, she hoped to distract Jesus from her living situation by bringing up the primary worship conflict of that time: "Our ancestors worshiped on this mountain, but you say that the place where people must worship is in Jerusalem." Refusing to take the bait, Jesus instead pointed her beyond the outward forms of worship to its true content: ". . . the hour is coming, and is now here, when the true worshipers will worship the Father in spirit and truth, for the Father seeks such as these to worship him. God is spirit, and those who worship him must worship in spirit and truth" (John 4:20-24).

God doesn't care whether we worship in Jerusalem or in Samaria, in a cathedral or a coffeehouse. God doesn't care whether we use pipe organs or rock bands, whether we wear robes or polo shirts, cross ourselves or raise our hands. What matters to God is whether or not we are opening all we are to him and giving ourselves back to him in love with heart, soul, mind, and strength. When we start to love the forms of worship more than the God to whom these forms direct us, then we have turned them into an idol.

> "What matters to God is whether or not we are opening all we are to him and giving ourselves back to him in love with heart, soul, mind, and strength."

I love chocolate. As kids, my sister and I always woke up on Easter morning to baskets filled with green grass and all kinds of sweets. I would immediately sift through the jellybeans, hard candy, and marshmallow puffs to find the real deal: chocolate. My favorite was always the chocolate formed in the shape of a bunny. At Christmastime we would also get chocolate, but it was formed in the shape of a Santa. Frankly, I didn't care what the shape was; all I cared about was the chocolate! Someone who turns up their nose at a chocolate Santa and says, "I only like bunnies!" obviously is not a lover of chocolate.

They care more about the outward *form* than its actual *content*. The same is true of many worshipers today.

God is calling us to become chocolate lovers again; people who love chocolate so much we could care less what shape it takes. The language we use, the style of our music, the order of our service, and the various elements we include are simply the means to a greater end. Ultimately, the content of worship is God himself. God is calling us to become Experiential Worshipers, so hungry for more of him that we are willing to open ourselves to whatever forms of worship are available. God is calling us to open ourselves to a more complete experience of him that will empower us to respond by expressing our love with heart, soul, mind, and strength.

FOR REFLECTION AND DISCUSSION

1. Have you ever had an experience of God that affected your thoughts, emotions, actions, and choices, like Isaiah did? How did it change you?

2. What do you mean when you use the word "worship"?

3. Have you ever confused the outward form of worship with its content (the chocolate)? Explain.

4. How would your worship change if you began to see every aspect of the service as an opportunity to experience God and respond to him?

5. Read John 4:5-26. Why do you think this woman brought up worship controversies when Jesus began addressing her personal life? What does it mean to worship God "in spirit and truth"?

Chapter 5

HeartWorship:
Loving God with Your ﹍ﹶﹶﹶﹶﹶﹶ

Unconditional Worship

It was a day like any other and Job was so grateful to be alive. "God is good" he thought to himself as he reflected on his many blessings: large flocks, faithful servants, a loving wife, and above all his ten precious children. Just the thought of them all gathered at the home of the eldest, celebrating another birthday, filled him with pride and joy. Sure it had taken hard work and persistence, but Job knew there were many factors beyond his control that had made his success possible. Weather patterns, market conditions, political stability, family support, and his own health; if he had been dealt different circumstances he probably would not have attained the status he now enjoyed. Job knew he was blessed and every day he thanked God whom he recognized as the source of all these good things.

Job's idyllic thoughts were rudely shattered by the sound of a worker from his farm approaching at a dead sprint. One look at the terror-stricken face and he knew there was serious trouble. The bad news came between gasps and sobs, "The Sabeans got every last ox and donkey and I am the only man to survive." While still taking this in, Job was interrupted by servant in dire straits. Haltingly he described a freak …ing storm that killed all of the sheep and all but one of …he shepherds. Before Job could ask for more details, yet another unwanted report came of three Chaldean raiding parties stealing the camels and killing all but one servant.

In one fell swoop Job's entire accumulated wealth, not to mention some of his best friends, had been ruthlessly stripped away. Reeling with shock and grief, the thought struck him that things simply could not get any worse, but then suddenly they did. The fourth and final messenger delivered the news every parent fears the most: "your sons and daughters are gone!" Tangled questions raced through his head faster than he could ask them: "How could a desert storm have collapsed their house? How did all of them die? Why did this have to happen? What could I have done to prevent it?"

In the maelstrom of sorrow that overcame him, Job expressed a grief no words could convey. He tore his robe, slid his knife out of the sheath, grabbed a handful of his own hair, and cut it to the roots. When his hair was gone and his tears were spent he collapsed on the ground, knowing instinctively what he had to do: offer whatever he had left to his God. "Naked I came from my mother's womb, and naked shall I return there; the LORD gave, and the LORD has taken away; blessed be the name of the LORD."

Sleep ended long before night and the temporary comfort of unconsciousness fled as sickening memories came flooding back. To this was added the excruciating pain of sores that had appeared over his entire body. Still, he praised his God. In her grief and confusion all his wife could say was, "Do you still persist in your integrity? Curse God, and die." He knew well the strain she was under, the burden of grief. But unable to stop himself, he blurted out, "You speak as any foolish woman would speak. Shall we receive the good at the hand of God, and not receive the bad?" Job had far more questions than answers, but there was one thing he was sure of: This was a time to turn toward God and not away from him. Deep in his heart, Job made the crucial choice to love and worship God, no matter what might come. (Based on Job 1)

To Do or Not to Do!

In his moment of crisis Job was faced with a crucial decision. He could curse God and die, as his wife suggested, or he could choose to worship God in spite of these tragic circumstances. Surely it is Job's greatest claim to fame that he courageously decided to worship God even in the midst of his grief and confusion! The point for us is clear; our *will* is a critical factor in our worship life. It constitutes our response to God's revelation. We make choices every day. Every decision, big or small, affects the course of our lives. How different would your life be if you had chosen a different school, profession, spouse, or faith? What an amazing and awe-full thing it was when the Creator endowed us with the power to choose! But why did God impart to each of us the risky responsibility of being a decision-maker? How much easier it would have been for God and for us if we had simply been kept under God's perfect control. We would still be enjoying the fruits of Eden in a blissful state of childlike innocence. Or would we? A closer look would reveal a glazed-over look in the eyes of those children, for they would not truly be children of God, but robots, puppets dangling at the end of a faultless string on a tidy stage.

I love my wife and two sons more than words can say. To live in a relationship of love with them is my greatest joy. I can guide my sons by my own example. I can make certain decisions for them. When they were younger I could even force them to obey me. But I cannot make them love me. Only they can choose love. Our Creator knew the price of authentic love was the risk of genuine choice. In order to make a relationship of real love possible, God gave us the freedom to accept or reject his love. Adam and Eve were given the power to choose, but tragically misused it and all of creation has been groaning ever since.

Now we live in the paradox of a world ruled by an almighty and purposeful God who has given us free will. This dilemma raises age-old questions: If God is truly omnipotent, how can we have the freedom to make real choices? Doesn't that violate God's absolute sovereignty? We live in a world broken by sin, but if there is no such thing as free will, who is responsible for sin—God? If God is perfectly good, how can he allow evil, sin, and death? This conundrum of free will vs. predestination is a debate that has continued unabated throughout the history of our faith.

This little book cannot solve these dilemmas, but we can consider the role of our will in worship, because Jesus called us to love God with all that we are, including our will. To love God with all our heart is to make a deliberate choice to give ourselves back to God in response to all he has given us. But remember, it is always the gracious initiative of God that empowers our freely given response. We cannot come

> "To love God with all our heart is to make a deliberate choice to give ourselves back to God in response to all he has given us."

to God or worship him of our own volition. God comes to us in love first. And while God's love empowers our response, it is still an invitation we are free to accept or reject. If God were to coerce our worship, it would be hollow and meaningless. Louie Giglio describes this dynamic when he writes, "Worship is our response to God. In other words we don't initiate worship, God does."[6]

Jesus emphasized the role of the will in authentic worship. In the Sermon on the Mount he said, "So when you are offering your gift at the altar, if you remember that your brother or sister has something against you, leave your gift there before the altar and go; first be reconciled to your brother or sister, and then come and offer your gift" (Matthew 5:23-24). It is one thing to go through the motions of making an offering. It is completely another thing to decide to go to someone you have wronged and seek reconciliation. Jesus is telling us deliberate acts of the will are a critical aspect of a healthy worship life.

Paul expressed the paradoxical tension between God's power and our will when he wrote, "Therefore, my beloved, just as you have always obeyed me, not only in my presence, but much more now in my absence, work out your own salvation with fear and trembling; for it is God who is at work in you, enabling you both to will and to work for his good pleasure" (Philippians 2:12-13). Paul boldly calls the Philippians to make concrete decisions regarding obedience and salvation. At the same time, Paul makes it clear that ultimately this is not their own doing—God is the one who is empowering them to make choices.

Everyday we walk into rooms and flip on light switches. We would never dream of taking credit for the light that is created. The power company provides the electricity; our part is to flip the switch. However, the power company does not force us to turn the lights on or off—that's our decision. The role of the will in worship is very much like this.

On the day of Pentecost the power of the Holy Spirit was poured out and the followers of Jesus were connected to the ultimate power source, just as we are today. The Holy Spirit empowered them to do things they could never have done before—things that ultimately changed the course of human history. Jesus anticipated this when he said, "The one who believes in me will also do the works that I do and, in fact, will do greater works than these, because I am going to the Father" (John 14:12). Look at those words again. When we put our trust in Jesus we can do what he did...and even more, because he comes alive in us. As Paul described it, "I have been crucified with Christ; and it is no longer I who live, but it is Christ who lives in me. And the life I now live in the flesh I live by faith in the Son of God, who loved me and gave himself for me" (Galatians 2:19-20).

When we experience the grace of God, through the power of the Spirit, we are connected to the source of power that fuels the sun and sustains the entire universe, but it is still up to us to flip the switch! When we are filled with the Spirit our will is not overwhelmed or negated. We are empowered to do amazing things; things we never would have dreamed of before. The Holy Spirit is the one who empowers us to choose HeartWorship.

Worship as Our Response

In the earliest books of the Bible, worship is primarily expressed as the deliberate choice to make a literal offering. Cain and Abel worshiped by offering grain and lambs to God. (Genesis 4:3-4). When Abram and Sarai first arrived in Canaan and received God's promise, they built an altar for offering (Genesis 12:7). God instructed the people of Israel to construct the Tabernacle while they were still in the wilderness so they would have a place of offering wherever they went (Exodus 25). Even in the New Testament we see Mary and Joseph making an offering at the dedication of their newborn child (Luke 2:24), Jesus commending a widow for the proportion of her financial offering (Luke 21:3), and Paul participating in sacrificial rites at the temple upon his return to Jerusalem (Acts 21:26). Like Job's decision to worship God in the midst of his pain, HeartWorship is based not on emotions, environment, or circumstance, but a deliberate decision to offer our whole selves to God.

The decision to attend a worship gathering or to set aside time in our daily schedule for individual worship is already an act of the will, an offering of our time and availability to God. This decision is so important because it opens us to a transforming encounter with God in which we can learn to love God more completely. In his pivotal book, *The Celebration of Discipline*, Richard Foster explains that we cannot, by our own willpower, change ourselves; only God can do this. The purpose of a spiritual discipline is that it creates an opportunity for God's Spirit to graciously do this life-changing work in us. He writes, "The Disciplines allow us to place ourselves before God so that he can transform us."[7] Foster goes on to explain that the spiritual discipline of worship "is our response to the overtures of love from the heart of the Father."[8]

Choosing to set aside time for worship is only the first of the choices we are called to make in worship. Luke describes the people's response after the very first Christian worship experience on the day of Pentecost: ". . . they were cut to the heart and said to Peter and to the other apostles, 'Brothers, what should we do?'" (Acts 2:37). What is the attitude of our hearts as we come to worship? Are we sitting back waiting for God to do something in us? Or are we asking the question, "What should we do?"

If we are to love God with all our soul, mind, and strength, we will need to learn to worship with deliberate decisions of the heart. The Experiential Worshiper understands genuine worship involves making conscious choices to seek God through everything we do in worship, receiving God as he reveals himself to us through every aspect of the experience, and responding with love, faith, commitment, and action.

> "The Experiential Worshiper understands genuine worship involves making conscious choices to seek God through everything we do in worship, receiving God as he reveals himself to us through every aspect of the experience, and responding with love, faith, commitment, and action."

When the people asked, "What should we do?" Peter said to them, "Repent, and be baptized every one of you in the name of Jesus Christ so that your sins may be forgiven; and you will receive the gift of the Holy Spirit" (Acts 2:38). The amazing thing is that they did it! The gracious nature of Peter's message, combined with the power of the Holy Spirit and willing hearts, resulted in literally thousands of transformed lives on that very first day of Christian worship. If we will open our hearts to God and be willing to respond with concrete choices, we will be transformed into Experiential Worshipers as well.

THE DECISIONS WE FACE

Your calendar reveals your most basic decisions about worship. How important is the weekly gathering with other Christians for worship? Some will say, "I'm too busy to go to church every Sunday!" They have clearly stated their decision to make other things more important in their lives than regularly gathering to worship God. Others will say, "I can worship God wherever I am. I don't need to go to church!" Of course this is true, but the question is whether they actually do worship God while they are in other places doing other things.

You can worship God anywhere, anytime, but you cannot become a complete worshiper by yourself. We need one another to learn how to worship God more fully wherever we are. The Spirit speaks to us through other people. We need community for support and accountability. Any part of the body cut off from the other members is incomplete. That is why from the very beginning Christians have gathered at least once a week to hear God's Word proclaimed, share the sacraments together, and worship God as a body in unity and love.

This is not about fulfilling some legalistic requirement; it is about getting and staying connected to the Source of life itself in order to live the life for which we were created. What is more important to you than gathering with others each week to worship God? Your honest answer will reveal to what extent you are beginning to choose to love God with your heart.

Having said that, it is also true Sunday is not the only day on your calendar that reveals your choices about worship. You cannot become a complete worshiper by worshiping just once a week. Too many of us go to the weekly gathering of our church and then cross worship off our "To Do" list, thinking we have completed the task. Weekly worship with others is meant to lead us into *daily* worship, alone with God. Don't let your worship life become like that old Las Vegas slogan: "What happens in church, stays in church!"

The more we learn to worship God as a deliberate choice, the more we will choose to worship him on a daily basis. This in turn will help us develop a lifestyle of worship in which we give all we are and all we do to God. Are you choosing to set aside time in your daily schedule exclusively to worship him? Imagine a child trying to grow on one meal a week. Imagine a couple trying to sustain a marriage on one hour a week. Experiential Worshipers choose to have private, one-on-one time with God in daily worship because they are hungry to love God with all their heart.

Once we have made the decision to set aside time to give ourselves to God, we need to consider the choices we are making *while* worshiping. What do you do when your mind wanders? Are you willing to try new ways of expressing your worship? How do you react when tears start to well up in your eyes? How do you respond when you feel challenged or offended by a certain scripture? What is your reaction when the pastor challenges you to make a public commitment? Do you silently complain about the things you don't like in the service or choose to focus on the God who is the reason for the gathering? Do you judge others from afar or choose instead to examine your own conscience in the loving presence of the God you worship?

These are the kinds of choices we all have to make in the midst of our worship experiences. However, worshiping God with our hearts does not end with the decisions we make *during* a time of worship, but continues with choices we make *afterward*. How does what you experienced in worship affect the rest of your day or even your life? Did what you hear go in one ear and out the other? Are you applying God's truth to your daily life? Are you following through with commitments you made during that gathering or did you forget about them once the music faded away? Are you willing to read books or study scripture to examine what God revealed to you during worship? Do the ways you treat people the other days of the week reflect the character of your time with God in worship? Loving God with all of your heart involves making choices before, during, and after intentional times of worship.

CHOOSING WORSHIP

After Joshua led the tribes of Israel into the Promised Land he gathered the people together at Shechem to clarify the choice he had made and what they, too, must decide: "Now if you are unwilling to serve the LORD, choose this day whom you will serve, whether the gods your ancestors served in the region beyond the River or the gods of the Amorites in whose land you are living; but as for me and my household, we will serve the LORD" (Joshua 24:15). Joshua understood worship begins with God's gracious initiative: promising them this land, leading them faithfully in obtaining it, blessing them with abundance. But he was also crystal clear that this initiative put before them a crucial choice: Whom will we worship? Whom will we serve? Will our encounter with God be reflected in every aspect of our lives?

We are constantly making choices either to genuinely love God with all that we are or to direct our attention instead to how we are feeling, what others might think of us, what is comfortable to us, what we are used to, or what will give us a sense of control. HeartWorship means choosing to move beyond these idols and give ourselves to God alone. HeartWorship means going beyond our circumstances and choosing, as Job did, to worship God no matter what. We cannot make this choice by our own strength, but the relentless grace of God in Jesus Christ frees us, and the indwelling presence of the Spirit empowers us to accept the invitation to this kind of worship feast.

> "HeartWorship means going beyond our circumstances and choosing, as Job did, to worship God no matter what."

In the chapters that follow we will be exploring what it means to worship God with our body, intellect, and emotions. Each of these critical aspects of worship is filled with decisions we have to make during and after worship gatherings. Will we read these words and go back to business as usual? Or will we make the deliberate choice to seek a more complete offering of ourselves to God in worship? As we allow the grace of God to transform us and the power of God's Spirit to fill us, we will find the resources we need to come to the table choosing to love God with all of our heart, soul, mind, and strength.

For Reflection and Discussion

1. What do you think of Job's decision to worship God in spite of all the tragedy in his life? What would you have done in his shoes?

2. What are some of the choices you make when you worship God? Are you conscious of all these decisions?

3. How can we grow in HeartWorship without slipping into legalism or ignoring the power of God?

4. How often do your experiences of God in worship lead you to make different choices in your life? How can this happen more regularly?

5. Read Acts 2:14-42. What moved those worshipers to ask Peter, "What should we do?" In what ways can you ask that same question in connection to your worship experiences?

Chapter 6

STRENGTHWORSHIP:
LOVING GOD WITH YOUR BODY

NO MORE DOUBTING

Thomas heard their words, but his mind couldn't accept what they said. His hopes had been sky high when they came into Jerusalem. The people shouted and waved palm branches, even laid their cloaks in the road. When Jesus got onto that donkey, Thomas knew that was it—Jesus would finally take his rightful place as king and lead his people to victory! But all that seemed a million miles away now. Jesus' cryptic words about going away, that terrible scene in the Garden of Gethsemane, the so-called "trial"—an obvious miscarriage of justice—and then the unthinkable: Jesus hanging naked on a cross. It seemed to Thomas like a nightmare from which he could not wake up. Hopes crushed, he vowed to himself never to be fooled like that again.

And now the other disciples were telling tales: "We have seen the Lord!" Come on, who did they think he was? He had eyes, didn't he? He had seen the nails driven through Jesus' wrists just like they had. He knew the soldier had thrust a spear into Jesus' side to confirm his death beyond a shadow of a doubt. There was no question he was gone and never coming back. Wishful words were not enough—he would need something much more than that, something tangible he could see and touch! "Unless I see the mark of the nails in his hands, and put my finger in the mark of the nails and my hand in his side, I will not believe."

A week went by and Thomas could not deny the change he saw in his friends. To a person, they were all sticking with the story they had seen Jesus alive. Thomas stubbornly persisted in his skepticism, but questions were creeping into the back of his mind: *If it was a delusion, why do they all agree? If they were making it up, why do they seem so different?*

His thoughts were interrupted by a commotion in the room. The others moved aside and there stood Jesus, undeniably alive and gloriously transformed! Doubts and unanswered questions melted away like mist before the rising sun. This was no ethereal ghost or delusion born in naive hope; this was the actual, physical man, the Jesus he had seen dying on the cross.

Finally something he could see and touch. Jesus looked at him, held out his arms, and spoke words that bored into Thomas' very heart and soul: "Put your finger here and see my hands. Reach out your hand and put it in my side. Do not doubt but believe." Awestruck, Thomas fell down in wonder and faith, worshiping: "My Lord and my God!" (Based on John 20:24-29).

GOD'S AFFIRMATION OF THE PHYSICAL

Too often history has condemned Thomas with the derogatory moniker "Doubting." We forget that none of the followers of Jesus believed in his resurrection until they had physical evidence they could see and touch. Jesus did not condemn Thomas for requesting a physical experience; he simply gave him what he needed. The truth is, we are physical beings and, like Thomas, physical experience is a necessary aspect of our encounters with God. Experiential Worshipers recognize loving God with all our strength means engaging in physical acts and offering our very bodies in worship.

> "Experiential Worshipers recognize loving God with all our strength means engaging in physical acts and offering our very bodies in worship."

From the beginning God affirmed the importance of the physical in our relationship with him. God's Word did not just remain an idea, but actually became what it described. God created our physical world and specifically told us its value: "It is very good" (Genesis 1:31). After sin marred that goodness, God did not give up on the world he created, but began working to redeem it. God made covenants with his people and used physical elements as signs of those renewed relationships: the rainbow with Noah, circumcision with Abraham, tablets of stone with Moses, animal sacrifices with Aaron. But somehow these signs were not enough. No matter how much patience God showed, we were not able to live in these covenants, even with their physical signs, so God went one step farther.

God didn't just *tell* us about himself, he *showed* himself to us. God entered into creation itself and became atoms and molecules, a tiny baby, a full-grown adult. The incarnation is God's definitive statement on the sacred character of redeemed creation. Jesus is the ultimate affirmation of our physical reality, because in him God became a flesh-and-blood person to redeem us, heart, soul, mind, and body. Jesus' ministry was largely taken up with touching the hurting and healing the sick. He demonstrated his deep concern for people's bodily well-being by his actions and explained such physical transformation is a sign of God's coming kingdom (Luke 4:16-18).

Above all, we see the sacred character of the physical in the fact that Jesus' body nailed to a cross achieved the redemption of all humanity. It was the reality of his resurrected body that vanquished the power of death. Paul makes it clear Jesus' death and resurrection not only opened the way for our salvation, but is God's means of redeeming the entire physical order: "the creation itself will be set free from its bondage to decay and will obtain the freedom of the glory of the children of God" (Romans 8:21).

When the first-century Christians in Corinth were busy trying to separate their spirituality from their physicality, Paul had to remind them in the clearest possible terms that, like the risen Christ, we will be resurrected with renewed *bodies* (1 Corinthians 15:12-57). The early church recognized the importance of this point by including the phrase "I believe . . . in the resurrection of the body" in the Apostles' Creed.

But the spiritual value of the body is not only a future promise. Paul tells us the indwelling presence of the Holy Spirit establishes once and for all the sacred character of the redeemed human body here and now: "Or do you not know that your body is a temple of the Holy Spirit within you, which you have from God, and that you are not your own? For you were bought with a price; therefore glorify God in your body" (1 Corinthians 6:19-20). Truly biblical spirituality is never divorced from our physicality, but always embraces the body as a sacred instrument of worship, designed to glorify God. This is why Dallas Willard says, "For good or evil, *the body lies right at the center of the spiritual life.*"[9]

The Body in Biblical Worship

Worshiping God with our bodies is not a new idea. Throughout the Bible, worship is described in physical terms. Both the primary Hebrew and Greek words for worship literally mean to fall down prostrate before someone. Many worship services today involve people's bodies only from the neck up, but biblical worship has always been a whole-body experience. Moses lay prostrate before God for forty days and nights (Deuteronomy 9:9-12); Ezekiel threw himself on the ground while interceding for the people (Ezekiel 11:13); Peter fell down before Jesus in recognition of his divinity (Luke 5:8).

The Psalms continually invite us into various physical expressions of worship: "*Clap* your hands, all you peoples; *shout* to God with loud songs of joy" (Psalm 47:1); "O come, let us worship and *bow down*, let us *kneel* before the LORD, our Maker!" (Psalm 95:6); "*Lift up your hands* to the holy place, and bless the LORD" (Psalm 134:2); "Let them praise his name with *dancing*" (Psalm 149:3). Obviously, David and the other psalmists understood the body as an indispensable instrument of worship. If they were not afraid to offer their bodies in physical acts of worship—why are we?

One of the most vivid examples of using the whole body as an instrument of praise took place when David returned the sacred Ark of the Covenant to the Holy City: "David and all the house of Israel were dancing before the LORD with all their might, with songs and lyres and harps and tambourines and castanets and cymbals" (2 Samuel 6:5). What is it that keeps us from expressing our love for God in such overtly physical ways? I think many of us are afraid that others will respond like David's wife Michal; when she saw David dancing before the Lord she "despised him in her heart" (2 Samuel 6:16).

Maybe we ourselves despise those whose physical acts of worship are not familiar to us. Those who kneel in worship tend to look down on those who lift up their hands, and vice versa. Those who clap sometimes judge those who cross themselves and vice versa. Why is that? I love David's reaction to Michal's disdain; he told her, "I will become even more undignified than this" (2 Samuel 6:22, NIV). Worship leader and songwriter Matt Redman invites us to respond with this same kind of holy boldness. In his insightful little book *The Unquenchable Worshiper*, Redman encourages us to become "undignified worshipers" who are unashamed to give our whole selves to God in worship, including our bodies, no matter what others might think.[10]

All of us have embraced our ears as receptors of God in worship. We listen to scripture, sermons, prayers, and music. Most of us have embraced the vocal cords as a bodily instrument of worship. We sing praises to God, pray out loud, and respond vocally with creeds, declarations, tongues, or liturgies, depending on our tradition. But there is so much more to the body than ears and vocal cords! Most of the time we are only engaging God with a small portion of our bodies. How liberating it is to recapture a more biblical view of the human body and its role in worship. Imagine the freedom that would come if we were willing to set aside our fears of what others might think, go outside our comfort zones, and learn to glorify God with all our physical strength.

LEARNING PHYSICAL WORSHIP

I can vividly remember that period in life when my feet did not touch the floor as I sat in the pew at church. My legs dangled freely over the edge and would swing back and forth almost effortlessly. No matter how many times my mom would remind me to stop, it was as if my legs had a mind of their own—I literally couldn't stop them from moving. Then my legs grew long enough so that, while they did not yet reach the floor, they did reach the back of the next pew. Now every time I swung my legs forward they would just barely brush the hymn rack in front of me—swish, swish—it made such a cool sound! My poor mother! How difficult it must have been to deal with a fidgety boy in a church culture where physical movement was frowned upon. There is a reason why Lutherans are sometimes referred to as the "frozen chosen"!

In some faith cultures, worship is viewed primarily as a neck-up activity: we worship with our brain and our vocal chords. The rest of the body is expected to stay pretty much motionless. For a physically-oriented person, that's like worshiping in a straitjacket! It was in youth group that I learned the whole body is an instrument of praise. Even though we were Lutherans, there the culture was different. We were encouraged to move around while we worshiped, to raise our hands, clap, do hand motions. Our youth director, Dave Herival, liked to say, "If you're happy, why don't you let your face know?" That was a novel idea to many of us, but when we tried it, we liked it!

What you do with your body has a direct and immediate impact on your thoughts, emotions, and decisions. Wherever you are right now, put down this book, stand up and stretch. Go ahead, do it. Done? Notice how you feel. Your mind is clearer. You feel better. You are ready to read more. Your body affects your heart, soul, and mind. When we kneel, fold our hands, and bow our heads we tend to feel humbled; our thoughts turn inward; we find ourselves more able to submit to God. When we stand, look upward, and stretch our open palms to the sky it tends to lift our emotions, focus our thoughts on God, and direct us toward thanks and praise.

There is a reason we usually teach children to close their eyes, fold their hands, and bow their heads when they pray. These are physical postures that help us focus all we are on God. It doesn't mean this is the only posture for prayer. In fact, the typical posture for prayer in the time of the New Testament was to stand, lift the hands, and look toward the sky. There is no one right posture for prayer or for worship. Different physical postures and motions affect us differently. When we learn to worship God physically, we discover that our body can help our heart, soul, and mind to love God more completely.

> "When we learn to worship God physically, we discover that our body can help our heart, soul, and mind to love God more completely."

BROADENING OUR PALATE OF PHYSICAL WORSHIP

I find it almost amusing that those who kneel and bow in worship tend to reject things like clapping and lifting hands during worship, while those who love to worship that way tend to look down on things like kneeling or bowing. These are just two different ways of doing the *same* thing—using your body to help you worship God more completely.

If you come from the clapping/hand-raising tradition, try kneeling and bowing. If you come from the kneeling/bowing tradition, try clapping and raising your hands. Of course it will feel awkward at first. You will wonder what others are thinking of you. But if you persist, focus on God, and say boldly with David, "I will become even more undignified than this," you will start to discover a wonderful new dimension to your worship experience. No matter what their tradition, Experiential Worshipers are hungry to use their bodies as instruments of praise in order to give themselves more fully to God.

Developing a broader repertoire of physical postures and movements in worship will help us encounter God more fully and keep us from falling into ruts and rote habits. Some will say, "But we don't do that kind of stuff in our church!" If so, then you will want to begin learning StrengthWorship during your private daily worship time. Be sure you have your daily time with God in a private place where you are free to express your love physically without feeling self-conscious. The next time you are worshiping God alone, try some different postures and see how they affect you.

- When you are confessing your sins to God, try kneeling and placing your hands over your face. This may help you get in touch with the shame and guilt you are carrying.
- As you accept God's forgiveness, try standing with upturned face, cupping your palms in front of you. This may help you receive more fully the cleansing flood of God's grace pouring over you.
- While you are giving glory and honor to God, try stretching your arms above your head with hands open. This may give you a deeper sense of how much you want to give yourself back to God.
- As you ask God to heal you and change your inner attitudes, try placing your palms over your heart and

applying gentle pressure. This may help you sense the transforming power of the Holy Spirit at work in you.

- When you ask God to lift your burdens or give you strength, try turning your open hands downward with each burden. This may help you release those struggles to God.

- While you pray for others, try lifting up your open palms in front of you. This may help you focus on lifting each of your loved ones to God as you pray for them.

- When giving thanks to God, try standing, placing your palms together in front of you, and bowing at the waist. This may give you a greater sense of gratitude for all that God has done in your life.

Are you getting the idea? The point is there is no one right physical posture for worship. Experiment. Figure out what postures help you the most in each particular aspect of worship. Keep trying new things. Refuse to get stuck in a rut. As you do this in private you will find greater courage to try it in public worship as well. If this kind of StrengthWorship is new to your church, start small. Simply placing your hands over your heart while singing will not distract anyone but may help you worship more fully. Holding your hands upturned in front of you is a step toward lifting your hands more completely. If you feel the dynamics in your church limit the possibilities for physical expression of worship, talk to your pastors and worship leaders in a positive way about it. If they are new to this aspect of biblical worship you might want to share with them my book on this topic written for leaders, *Experiential Worship* and the churchwide campaign kit that goes along with this book.[11]

There are other ways to expand the physical aspect of your worship life. When you are sitting in a public worship space, notice the visual images and symbols around you. Maybe there is a cross in the front or other ancient symbols designed into the walls or windows. Maybe there are banners on the walls or screens with projected images. Whatever the visual environment, learn to focus on the symbols that will help you worship more fully. When I am singing about Jesus' sacrifice or hearing the words of forgiveness pronounced to me, I like to look at the large cross in the front of our worship space. It helps me move beyond the words to experience more completely what Christ did for me. When I am singing about God's greatness or power, I like to look out the high windows in our building to see the limitless sky above, a reminder of God's limitless character. What are the images around you that can draw you more fully into an encounter with God?

Becoming more aware of other physical aspects in a service can enhance your worship experience. When I am listening to a sermon I like to hold an open Bible in my lap to remind me of the source of the message. When I am worshiping with my family, I like to hold my wife's hand or put an arm around one of my sons, a reminder of the blessing of the family of faith. When receiving communion I focus on the connection between the elements of bread and wine and the body and blood of Jesus, broken for my redemption. As I taste those elements I try to taste God's goodness. As I swallow and feel the elements moving inside of me I reflect on the intimacy of God's Spirit in my life. During the prayer time I like to give attention to my breathing, exhaling as I release things to God, drawing breath in as I receive God's goodness. When I am standing and listening to the blessing at the end of our service, I like to take a deep breath and hold it for a moment, exhaling slowly as I feel God's blessing surround me. What can you do with your body in worship to help you give yourself to God more completely?

Of course there is a balance we need to seek as we learn to worship God with our bodies. We must be sensitive to the effects our actions have on others without worrying about what they are thinking about us. The more we take the focus off ourselves and place it onto God, the more we will be free to become "undignified worshipers" in the tradition of David. However, we don't want to distract others, draw unnecessary attention to ourselves, or turn away newcomers in our midst. Paul instructs us to express our worship in a way that invites unbelievers into our midst so that they might experience God. Then, describing physical worship, Paul says, "that person will bow down before God and worship him, declaring, 'God is really among you'" (1 Corinthians 14:25).

OFFER YOUR BODY

During that year we lived in Jerusalem, my wife and I shared an apartment in the heart of the walled Old City. It was directly across from the ancient church that is built over the rock of Golgotha and the empty tomb of Joseph of Arimathea. Early each morning I would stop in the small chapel at Golgotha for my quiet time. As I watched humble Greek nuns and pilgrims from all over the world unashamedly worshiping Jesus with their whole bodies, I found my own Scandinavian inhibitions melting away. Kneeling there on stones worn smooth by centuries of bended knees, smelling the incense, seeing the candlelit icons, bowing down to the floor in awe, lighting a prayer candle, touching the actual rock where Jesus died, I experienced God's presence in a unique and wonderful way. The reality of Jesus' suffering, the precious gift of atonement, and the power of his resurrection all became more real to me through the physical aspects of worshiping in that unique place.

This experience has given me a passion for worshiping God with my body no matter what setting I am in. No more "neck-up" worship for me—I'm too hungry for more of God! Are you willing to break through your inhibitions and offer your body more completely to God in worship? The good news is you don't need to go to Jerusalem to love God with all your strength, but you do need to be stretched out of your comfort zones. You do need to be willing to try new things in order to experience God with your body as well as your heart, soul, and mind. Experiential Worshipers are always exploring what it means to glorify God more completely with their bodies.

FOR REFLECTION AND DISCUSSION

1. Why do you think Jesus didn't condemn Thomas for asking for physical evidence of his resurrection, but offered it to him instead?

2. How does the physicality of Jesus' birth, ministry, death, and resurrection affect your view of the role of our bodies in our spiritual life?

3. Do you feel any inhibitions when you think of dancing before the Lord like David did? What do you think it would take to move in that direction toward greater freedom?

4. What kind of physical postures help you to experience God more fully in worship? What might be some new postures that will help you grow into a more complete worshiper?

5. Read 2 Samuel 6:1-16. What do you think moved David to dance before the Lord? Why do you think Michal despised him for this? How can you overcome the fear that others might despise you for using your body more fully in worship?

Chapter 7

MindWorship:
Loving God with Your Thoughts

From Unknown to Known

Athens! The ancient capitol of wisdom and learning formed the foundations of western civilization. Paul felt a long way from Tarsus, where the temples and monuments of his hometown were modeled after the architecture of this great city. The age-old Parthenon, perched atop the Acropolis and casting its imposing shadow over this birthplace of Greek philosophy, appeared to challenge even the grandeur of Jerusalem, with its towering Temple Mount. As he walked through the market at the city's center, Paul's agile mind was buzzing with thoughts sparked by the sights surrounding him. In every direction stood a different temple to yet another god of the Greek and Roman pantheon. A strong passion rose inside of him as he gazed upon this orgy of idolatry, aware of his growing desire to unfetter minds that had been imprisoned by myth and human invention.

Day after day Paul had addressed the leaders of the Jewish synagogue there in Athens and tried to show from the Scriptures that Jesus is the long-awaited Messiah. He was shocked by their unwillingness to even consider what he had to say. Perhaps their minds had been hardened in the face of the pagan philosophies they had to confront every day in this most intellectual of cities. Paul's attempts to proclaim the good news in the Athenian marketplace had been just as much an uphill battle. The Epicurean and Stoic philosophers Paul met there seemed unable to comprehend what he kept trying so hard to explain. Gradually he realized their whole frame of reference was so different he could no longer rely on his familiar strategy of quoting the Hebrew prophets and referring to the Law of Moses to make a case for Jesus' divinity. He knew he needed a different approach.

Passing by an altar labeled "To an unknown god," Paul allowed himself a wry smile. "Not taking any chances," he thought to himself, and then pondered the irony of so much human wisdom and religion, and yet so little knowledge of the true God. Suddenly it hit him: this was the approach he'd been looking for. His pulse quickened as he ascended the hill of the Areopagus. One of the Epicureans had invited him to address the famous philosophical council of Athens—an unprecedented opportunity to proclaim the gospel to the leading thinkers of the city.

Looking out over the learned faces of the council, Paul took a deep breath and began: "Athenians, I see how extremely religious you are in every way. For as I went through the city and looked carefully at the objects of your worship, I found among them an altar with the inscription, 'To an unknown god.' What therefore you worship as unknown, this I proclaim to you." The words were beginning to flow and Paul felt his strength building as he went on to describe the holiness and compassion of the God whom they had so long known in vague shadows and heard in distant echoes. He threw in a couple of quotes from the Greek poets he had read and saw a flash of recognition pass over some faces. After pointing out the futility of idol worship, Paul concluded by calling for repentance and inviting them to put their trust in the Jesus who conquered death through his resurrection—the "unknown God" who has made himself unmistakably known.

Paul was used to the reactions that came when he proclaimed the resurrection—a stumbling block to Jews and folly to Gentiles. Some of the council openly scoffed at the claim that Jesus had risen from the dead. "Nonsense!" "Impossible!" But others were intrigued by the compelling logic of Paul's argument and invited him to return the next day for more discussion. As he was getting ready to leave, a man named Dionysius, a member of the Areopagus, silently approached Paul and pulled him into a private corner. In conspiratorial tones he confided to Paul that he had always sought the unknown god because he sensed there must be more than the Greek myths he had grown up with. He told Paul in a whisper, "When you were speaking it suddenly became clear to me. I believe what you said is true and I want to find out how to become a follower of this Jesus." Thrilled, Paul invited him to join the other believers in Athens for a time of worship and made arrangements to meet with him afterward to talk more about his fledgling faith. (Based on Acts 17:16-34)

COMPREHENDING GOD

From the beginning of human memory, people searched for their Creator. Intrigued by the mystery, they reached out for the unknown God, constructing myths and religions to fill the void. Noble as these human attempts were, it was only when God broke the silence and spoke to people like Noah and

Abraham and Moses that the impenetrable shroud was pulled back. No longer was God a distant concept, shaped by imagination, superstition, and extrapolation. Now God spoke directly, clearly: "I have set my bow in the clouds," "I will make of you a great nation," "I AM WHO I AM" (Genesis 9:13; 12:2; Exodus 3:14). These revelatory moments were more the exception than the rule, but they formed markers on the path to a limited understanding of God.

The Hebrew Scriptures chronicle the initiative of God revealing himself to humanity through words, recorded and passed down through the centuries. Powerful and illuminating as they were, these words of divine self-disclosure were not enough, so God took the next step. John opens his gospel: "In the beginning was the Word, and the Word was with God, and the Word was God . . . And the Word became flesh and lived among us . . ." (John 1:1, 14).

The miracle of the Word is that the ineffable God of the universe became comprehendible by expressing himself in human language and as a human being in Jesus. John used the Greek term *logos*, laden with philosophical inference, to capture the truth we have a God who not only speaks, but a God who makes himself comprehensible to the human intellect. God has chosen to express himself in rational, reasonable terms, so we might come to know and understand him with our minds.

> "God has chosen to express himself in rational, reasonable terms, so we might come to know and understand him with our minds."

At the same time, *who God is* far exceeds our ability to comprehend. As Paul says, "God's foolishness is wiser than human wisdom, and God's weakness is stronger than human strength"

(1 Corinthians 1:25). Yet God squeezed himself into human language and "emptied himself" in the person of Jesus Christ, so that as we "search for God and perhaps grope for him" we might be able to find him (Philippians 2:7; Acts 17:27). In the written words of scripture and the living Word—Jesus—God has measured out a thimble-sized portion of himself so our cups might be filled to overflowing with his grace and truth. The good news Paul so effectively proclaimed to the Athenian philosophers is that the "unknown god" has become for us the God who can be known, even through our finite human intellect!

FROM WORDS TO UNDERSTANDING

The third oldest member of our family is Lulu, an Amazon parrot. Lulu's vocabulary is amazing. As soon as she sees the food come out she begins to talk. "Good morning!" "How are you today?" "Are you a good girl or a baaaad girl?" But when she is really serious about getting a treat she brings out the big guns. We ask in a singsong voice, "What do you say to the Lord?" and she responds with exaggerated enthusiasm by singing a pitch-perfect rendition of the "Hallelujah Chorus" from Handel's *Messiah*. It sounds so good that at first you believe her. You get the feeling she means it. Then reason takes over and you realize she is just mimicking sounds and has no idea what she is actually singing.

Too often our worship slips into just this—mimicking sounds while losing sight of what those sounds really mean. We sing "Hallelujah!" but do we really know what we are saying? When we get in the rut, go through the motions, and let our mind wander we are really no different than Lulu. Jesus' great commandment calls us from merely parroting words to intentionally engaging God with our deepest thoughts and most profound understanding.

Have you ever put your foot in your mouth only to remember the old saying, "Do not operate mouth until brain is engaged"? Have you ever arrived home and not been able to remember actually driving there? Scary, huh? Operating the body without engaging the mind can be a dangerous thing. Pretending to worship God without engaging your mind is equally hazardous. It doesn't matter what we are saying or doing in worship if we don't know what it means. You probably heard of the little boy who began the Lord's Prayer, "Our Father, who art in heaven, Harold be thy name." A young girl continued, "Give us this day our jelly bread." Another boy pleaded, "Deliver us from weevils." When we don't know the meaning of the words we are speaking, we can end up saying almost anything.

It should come as no surprise Jesus called us to love God with all of our *mind*. God is not interested in mindless worship. If we are not engaged intellectually, anything else we do will be meaningless, for the mind is where we register the meaning of our actions. Paul explained this to the Corinthians when they were over-emphasizing the gift of tongues in worship, "For if I pray in a tongue, my spirit prays but my mind is unproductive. What should I do then? I will pray with the spirit, but I will pray with the mind also; I will sing praise with the spirit, but I will sing praise with the mind also" (1 Corinthians 14:14-15). In Romans 12:2 Paul described the impact of "reasonable" worship this way, "Do not be conformed to this world, but be transformed by the renewing of your minds, so that you may discern what is the will of God—what is good and acceptable and perfect." When our *minds* are engaged in worship we learn to discern God's will for our lives, we are renewed so we begin to think differently, and our whole selves enter into a process of transformation. Experiential Worshipers always seek discernment and renewal by offering their minds to God as an act of worship.

> "When our *minds* are engaged in worship we learn to discern God's will for our lives, we are renewed so we begin to think differently, and our whole selves enter into a process of transformation."

MINDING OUR WORSHIP

Once I attended a worship service at a large, growing congregation. The facilities were state-of-the-art, the logistics of the service were well organized, and the music was excellent. I laughed at the humorous drama. I was moved by a story. I felt good as I was clapping and singing upbeat songs. "What a great service," I remarked as we drove away, but then it suddenly hit me . . . I could not say what the service was actually about. I could describe the various elements of the service, but I could not identify the meaning of those elements. Somehow I had managed to go through the motions of worship without engaging God with my mind. Sometimes we are bored with a worship service and allow our minds to wander and be distracted by things that are far from God. Other times we are enjoying the various aspects of the service so much that we focus on *what* we are doing rather than *why* we are doing it. Either way, we have missed the point.

If we want to love God with all our mind we will intentionally focus our thoughts on preparing ourselves for worship.

This can begin long before we ever arrive at church or our community's gathering place.

- Are you thinking about being with others for worship the night before or the day of the service?
- If your church makes the information available, are you aware of what the topic or scripture will be for that week?
- Are you developing a sense of anticipation by reflecting on what God will do in your life and in your church during that time?
- As you travel to the church are you beginning to focus your mind on an encounter with God?
- As you enter the property do you have a sense of pilgrimage to a holy encounter?
- As you come into the building is it with an expectation of transformation?
- As you wait for the service to begin are you praying, asking God to prepare you and open your mind to the truth that will set you free?

In other words, are you engaging God with your mind? If not, then you will not be able to worship God fully with your thoughts.

If we seek to love God with all our mind we will intentionally focus our thoughts on the meaning of what we are doing in worship. What is the very first thing that happens in your worship service? Where are your thoughts at that moment? Are you looking around to see who is or isn't there? Are you wondering how your new outfit looks to others? Are you wondering what the score is in the ball game you are missing? Or are you focused on the meaning of the words conveyed by the opening reading, the opening song, or the introduction to the service? Loving God with all our mind means continually redirecting our thoughts from the myriads of distractions back to focus on the God we have gathered to worship.

FOCUSING OUR MIND IN WORSHIP

It is amazing how easily our minds can wander during worship. As a pastor who leads four worship gatherings every Sunday, I understand the battle well. By the third and fourth services it is easy for me to switch on the autopilot and think about other things. Sometimes I even find myself thinking about what I am going to preach the following Sunday! But, as I grow as an Experiential Worshiper, the Spirit empowers me to deliberately redirect my thoughts toward him as the object of my affection and attention. When I am able to do this I often find the fourth worship service to be the most fulfilling because I am finally able to focus on God and give him everything.

The distractions we face in worship are sometimes of our own making and other times not. Without becoming superstitious, it is important to acknowledge there are powers at work that want to keep us from focusing our thoughts on God in worship. Paul explains his approach this way: "Indeed, we live as human beings, but we do not wage war according to human standards; for the weapons of our warfare are not merely human, but they have divine power to destroy strongholds. We destroy arguments and every proud obstacle raised up against the knowledge of God, and we take every thought captive to obey Christ" (2 Corinthians 10:3-5). This is why prayer is so important in our preparation, asking God to take every thought captive to worship him. This is why we need to ask for the Spirit's help to continually turn our mind back to God when other things draw us away.

When you are singing a familiar hymn or song it is easy to just enjoy the music and let it carry you along. But when you do, remember Lulu singing "Hallelujah!" Don't just parrot the words. Think about what you are singing. Picture the things those words are describing. Direct your expression of praise and wonder specifically to God the Father or Jesus or the Holy Spirit. Imagine the myriads of angels and heavenly creatures leading the song you are singing. See yourself in the midst of people from all over the planet and throughout history joining in one eternal anthem of praise. Think about the aspects of God described by the lyrics. Reflect on what that means in your relationship with him. Consider what this might mean for your life beyond the worship service. While you sing, use physical postures like those described earlier to help you keep your mind connected to the meaning of the words.

As you join others in liturgy or corporate prayer, engage your mind with the meaning of the words just as you engage your mouth with their sounds. Think about what you are saying and notice the power of saying those things together with your brothers and sisters in Christ. If you are joining in a creed or profession of faith, consider the strength and support of the community when your own faith feels weak and wavering. If you are joining in a prayer composed by someone else, notice the wisdom born of that person's spiritual experience and seek to gain insight from it in your own worship life. If you are speaking ancient words, remember you are just part of the history of God's work on this planet and appreciate the privilege of joining your voice with the "great cloud of witnesses" that have gone before us.

When you hear the scriptures being read, open a Bible so you can follow along and see its context. If it is a narrative text, picture the people being described and imagine their setting. Ponder what each one would have been thinking and feeling as the events unfolded. Notice what God was doing in those events and put yourself into the story. If it is prose, focus on following the flow of the ideas described. What is the truth being communicated and what does this mean in your life today?

As the sermon begins, focus on listening for God's voice speaking to you through the words of the preacher. If they tell a story, enter into the story with them. If they relate their message to current events, consider the connection to your world and your life. If they bring in other Scriptures, look for the points of contact. If they suggest application ideas, imagine how your life would be different if you began to live out this truth every day. See if you can follow the direction of the message. How do these elements of the sermon fit together? Where is the preacher going with this? What is the Spirit saying to me? What is the transforming truth being offered? How might I be different if this truth sets me free? Remember preaching is a two-way street—the quality of any sermon is as dependent on how fully you engage your mind with the message and open yourself to the Spirit as it is on the preacher's skill and effort.

If you are receiving communion, ask God to prepare your heart to receive him more fully through the physical elements. As you hear the words Jesus spoke at the Last Supper, imagine what it would have been like to be in that upper room with him. If you go up to the front to receive the elements, think about what that action of going forward means to you. If the elements are passed to you, think about what it means for you to be served in that way. As you see others receiving this same gift, reflect on your connection to each other in the body of Christ. As you chew and swallow, think about the love that caused Jesus to accept torture and death on your behalf. As you feel those elements going deep inside you, consider just how close the Holy Spirit is to you at that moment. As you taste the goodness of those elements, celebrate the joy of the resurrection and that day when we will eat and drink with Jesus in his eternal kingdom!

If you are part of a worship gathering where someone is being baptized, take the opportunity to claim the promises of your own baptism anew. As you watch what is happening, remember that God came to you with his grace before you could even respond to him. Ask the Holy Spirit to fill you with the faith of a child. Reflect on Jesus' call to follow him and recall what it was like when you first began to answer that invitation. As you think about your own baptism, remember to recommit your life to this walk with Jesus every day.

When the offering is being received, think about your finances and intentionally commit them to God's purposes. Think about what that money will be used for and ask God to bless it. If there is time for reflection use it to reflect. Offer to God whatever is on your mind at that moment. Take that opportunity to pray about what the Holy Spirit has been revealing to you during the service. If a special song is sung, listen to the words and ask God to speak to you. If announcements are given, consider each opportunity and ask the Spirit to show you how he would have you participate. If there are other responses you are invited to make during the service, focus your mind on responding as fully as possible. If a benediction is spoken at the end of the service, imagine Jesus making these words a reality for you personally. If you are sent out with a final charge, ask yourself what God is sending you out to do the rest of the week.

Connecting Intellectually

When I was sixteen years old my sister, Leslie, and I took a month-long car trip through Europe. On the very first evening of our adventure we drove into the West German town of Bayreuth in our Volkswagen Beetle. For the first time in our young lives we were faced with the daunting task of survival. If we did not find a place to stay, we would not have a bed that night. If we did not find a place to eat, we would not have dinner that night. Our initial attempts to find the local youth hostel were unsuccessful, so Leslie finally convinced me to ask directions from a pedestrian. I rolled down the window and, in a well-rehearsed German phrase, asked for directions. The man on the sidewalk assumed I could actually speak German and proceeded to let forth a torrent of guttural Germanic sounds unlike anything I had ever heard. I nodded, smiled, and rolled up the window as we drove away. After a moment of silence Leslie asked, "Well, what did he say?" I turned to her and said, "I have no idea." I was too embarrassed to admit that I couldn't understand him and as a result we were still lost.

Many of us are too embarrassed to admit we don't understand what is happening in worship, or in the Scriptures, or what our pastor is talking about, and all we do is smile, roll up the window, and drive away, missing out on what God wants to give us. Or maybe we are too distracted for our minds to connect with what God is doing. Sometimes we are simply lazy and end up just going through the motions. No wonder so many people complain that worship is boring! When our mind is not engaged with God, worship is literally meaningless. Experiential Worshipers are so hungry for meaning-full worship they intentionally seek to love God with all of their mind, and apply everything that God has given them to get there.

> "When our mind is not engaged with God, worship is literally meaningless."

For Reflection and Discussion

1. Have you ever parroted words in worship while your mind was somewhere else? Why does that happen so often?

2. Do you think comprehending truth is important to the quality of your worship life? Why or why not?

3. How can we worship God with our minds when God is infinite and ultimately incomprehensible?

4. What do you plan on doing to specifically engage your mind more fully as you worship God?

5. Read Romans 12:1-2. In what way does more complete worship lead to "the renewing of your minds"? How can worship help you "discern what is the will of God—what is good and acceptable and perfect"?

Chapter 8

SoulWorship:
Loving God with Your Emotions

Tears in Action

Holding the small alabaster flask of perfumed oil tightly in her hand, she hurried toward Simon's house remembering the day her mother had given it to her. "It's for your wedding day, my child," her mother had whispered as she pressed it in her palm. Ever since that day she had guarded it as her most precious possession, made even more so now because it was the only thing of her mother's that remained. Yet, since the first time she heard the rabbi from Nazareth, even more precious to her than the perfume was the love and mercy that bathed her when he spoke. Skeptical at first, her soul soared with hope when Jesus described a kingdom where sinners could be set free and broken people made whole. And it wasn't just words; with her own eyes she had seen him heal people and set them free—people like her!

She had only ever heard condemnation from religious leaders before, especially from Simon the Pharisee who openly denounced her before the entire village. She never denied her sins; she knew her father's abuse and her mother's early death were no justification for the life she had lived. Yet her heart had always longed for something better and now Jesus was offering exactly that. Somehow the authority and power of his words moved her to respond and more than once she had tried to tell him so, but the crowd was always too thick. *This is my chance,* she thought as she saw the lights and heard the voices streaming from the windows of Simon's house.

Slipping in among the servants, she stepped into the room and saw the men reclining around the low, three-sided table. Simon was stretched out at the head of the table with Jesus beside him in the place of honor. She saw the look of disgust on Simon's face as he caught sight of her, but before he could say anything, she rushed to Jesus' feet. Opening her mouth to deliver her well-rehearsed speech, words would not come. Emotions she could not begin to describe welled up from within, choking her ability to speak. Instead she collapsed, sobbing at his feet. Through blurry eyes she saw her tears falling onto Jesus' dusty feet and without a second thought she began to untie her hair and wipe them clean.

Once the tears stopped she tried to sit up and look him in the eye to deliver her speech, but all she could do was cling to those beautiful, untouchable feet. Knowing the weight of her shame would keep her from reaching his head, she suddenly knew what she must do. Breaking open the precious vial, she began to kiss Jesus' feet and pour out the pungent oil. Rubbing in the oil and gently massaging, she tried to tell by her actions what no words could say. Then Jesus began to speak, not to her, but to Simon. He told a story of debts owed and love shown. She wasn't sure exactly what it meant until Jesus took her hand, lifted her to her feet, and told Simon that hers was the greater love. Indescribable feelings of joy and hope and freedom—feelings she had never known—flooded her soul as he looked in her eyes and spoke the words that would ring in her heart forever, "Your sins are forgiven." (Based on Luke 7:36-50)

THE POWER OF EMOTION

Emotions are one of the most powerful forces in human experience and can dramatically shape the nature and direction of our lives. This woman was so deeply moved by Jesus' message of grace and forgiveness she overcame her shame and made a dramatic offering of love to Jesus. That offering involved an intellectual understanding of the good news of the kingdom, a brave act of the will, a controversial physical act of worship, but also a tearful expression of powerful emotions. Often we are suspicious of emotions and many have questioned the validity of emotional expression in worship. However, this unnamed woman offers us a vivid example of what it means to love Jesus with all of the heart, soul, mind, and strength. In this dramatic act of devotion she underscores for us the importance of engaging our emotions in complete, biblical worship.

Many of us like to think of ourselves as primarily rational beings, and yet emotions often have a bigger impact on our lives than purely rational decisions. We all act in irrational ways. How many times have you considered a purchase you knew you couldn't afford, but made it anyway? How many things have you said in the heat of the moment you didn't mean and wished you could take back? If reason ruled our lives, there would be no need for psychologists, marriage counselors, and twelve-step groups.

Children are a wonderful reminder of our emotional nature because they have not yet learned to mask their feelings as adults have. Kids laugh, cry, scream with rage, and squeal with delight, all in the space of a few moments. You can watch the emotions play across their little faces like storms on a lake. As adults we can look back and see what an important role feelings have played in our lives. My most memorable moments were all deeply emotional experiences: getting my horse, my first date, the death of my grandparents, playing for the state football championship, high school graduation, my wedding, the birth of my children, my ordination, my best friend's suicide, the birth of my long-awaited nephew, my son's graduation . . . the list goes on and on.

If emotions play a part in the most important events of our lives, why would we ignore this aspect of human experience when expressing our love to God? In an overly rational age we are told faith is to be built on fact, not feeling, and so expressing emotions in worship is considered by some irresponsible, if not heretical. The result is bland, lifeless worship which, while perhaps faithful to a certain kind of doctrine, never moves us to loving God with our soul. Maybe we find comfort in a controlled intellectual exercise or formal ritual practice safely devoid of any real passion. And yet when we read the scriptures we notice a profound contrast between our bland worship and the passionate, holistic expressions of love for God modeled by biblical people.

"In an overly rational age we are told faith is to be built on fact, not feeling, and so expressing emotions in worship is considered by some irresponsible, if not heretical."

EMOTIONS OF BIBLICAL PROPORTIONS
"How long must I bear pain in my soul, and have sorrow in my heart all day long? . . . Turn to me and be gracious to me, for I am lonely and afflicted . . . Weeping may linger for the

night, but joy comes with the morning . . . You have turned my mourning into dancing; you have taken off my sackcloth and clothed me with joy, so that my soul may praise you and not be silent . . . May those who sow in tears reap with shouts of joy." (Psalms 13:2; 25:16; 30:5, 11-12; 126:5)

Even a cursory reading of the Psalms reminds us biblical worship is a profoundly emotional experience, incorporating both songs of celebration and songs of lament. There is no "stiff upper lip" here—the feelings of the soul are embraced as a vital part of the language of worship. The psalmists repeatedly invite us to express our love to God with strong emotion. Notice the great spectrum of emotions represented: sorrow to joy, weeping to rejoicing. There is no screening out "unacceptable" feelings; the soul is laid bare for God to see. The Psalms call us to rediscover emotional honesty as a vital part of authentic worship. In his book, *A Sacred Sorrow,* Michael Card writes, "The Scriptures are filled with lament. Every major biblical character, from Abraham to Paul, is heard praying their protests to God . . . Our personal worship experience is not complete unless we understand the lost language of lament."[12]

The Scriptures are filled not only with lament, but expressions of genuine feeling from every part of the emotional spectrum. An aging and childless Abraham expressed his fear and despair to God (Genesis 15). The people of Israel "wept before the LORD" for entire days as an act of worship when facing civil war with the tribe of Benjamin (Judges 20). When Hezekiah reestablished temple worship in Jerusalem the people were having such a good time they extended the seven-day festival another seven days (2 Chronicles 30:22-23). When Jesus saw the grief of Mary over her brother Lazarus, "he was greatly disturbed in spirit and deeply moved . . . Jesus began to weep" (John 11:33-35). Jesus said to his disciples, "I have said these things to you so that my joy may be in you, and that your joy may be complete" (John 15:11). The disciples expressed fear in the face of a Galilean storm, became angry at the arrogance of the brothers Zebedee, and celebrated their success upon returning from their mission trip (Mark 4:40; 10:41; Luke 10:17). Entering the temple courts, Jesus' righteous anger fueled his radical overturning of the tables (Matthew 21:12). In the garden of Gethsemane, Jesus was so afraid of the suffering awaiting him that "in his anguish he prayed more earnestly, and his sweat became like great drops of blood" (Luke 22:44). On Easter morning when the women arrived at the tomb they were "terrified" by an angelic messenger and left the empty tomb "with fear and great joy" (Luke 24:5; Matthew 28:8). Jesus had promised his followers this full range of emotional experiences: "Very truly, I tell you, you will weep and mourn, but the world will rejoice; you will have pain, but your pain will turn into joy" (John 16:20).

Whatever our predisposition toward emotion, it is impossible to deny that feelings comprise a major aspect of who we are as human beings and play a significant role in our faith. The Bible is not simply a logical account of historical facts and theological ideas, but also a passionate love story, filled with every kind of human experience and emotion. This is not to say that our worship of God should be based on our emotional state at any given moment. Earlier we saw Job as the model for determination to worship God as a choice, regardless of feelings or circumstance (Job 1:20). Obviously, feelings can never be a substitute for the intellectually ascertained basis of our faith or the Spirit-empowered decision to trust the truth revealed to us, but to separate our worship from this critical aspect of human experience is to rob worship of its biblical passion and radically reduce its relevance to our lives.

THE IMPACT OF THE SOUL

"I want to keep coming, but I just can't anymore." She was a woman who had been attending our church for a month or two. Having only greeted her after worship a few times, I didn't know anything about her, so I was unsure why she had asked to meet with me in my office. "Why can't you keep coming?" I asked. She started to answer, then stiffened. In spite of her best efforts I could see a lone tear beginning to make its way silently down her left cheek. I pushed the well-used tissue box toward her and she took one, burying her face in it like she was hiding. I waited while she regained her composure. "I don't know what it is, but every Sunday in church I just start to cry."

Somehow encountering a God who loved her unconditionally touched something deep inside that could only be expressed through tears. However, the shame she felt in openly showing emotion during worship was so great it was driving her away from the very thing she longed for the most. I explained that emotions are a good gift, a God-given way for us to open our soul in worship, a source of healing, and a means of growth as Christ-followers. My words didn't instantly change the shame she felt in crying, but they did give her the courage to continue expressing her feelings to God in worship.

Something intense happens when our emotions come together with our body, intellect, and will in

> "Something intense happens when our emotions come together with our body, our intellect, and our will in worship."

worship. We *know* that we are sinful, but when we *feel* remorse this moves us to genuine repentance. We *sing* the words of celebration, but when we *feel* the hope of salvation we find strength to face our deepest struggles. We *hear* the call to discipleship, but when we *feel* inspired, it leads us to commit ourselves to a life of service. Emotions can connect our intellect with our will like nothing else. We have all heard stories of people who, in a moment of mortal crisis, showed superhuman strength by lifting a car off an injured person or some other amazing feat. Our emotions can move us to do things we otherwise would never do.

Experiential Worshipers embrace emotion as an indispensable aspect of worship and develop a growing hunger to offer themselves to God with a passionate love song that rises from the depths of the soul. As we intentionally learn how to express our love to God emotionally, we will discover even greater potential for our lives to be transformed through worship.

LEARNING EMOTIONAL EXPRESSION

I remember one night as a kid watching my sister across the dinner table from me, spooling spaghetti onto her fork. I don't know what got us started, but we had been giggling—uncontrollably. Pasta-sauce-out-the-nose kind of giggling. Our parents had taken about as much of this as they could handle. Their threat involved a one-way trip to the bedroom with no meal service and a hint of corporal punishment on the side. An uneasy silence had fallen over the table. I was employing all my underdeveloped willpower not to look up at my sister. *Focus on chewing and swallowing*, I told myself over and over, as I twirled another mouthful onto my fork and popped it in my mouth. One glimpse of my sister's gleaming eyes and twitching facial muscle was all it took for the bubble to burst. I'm not sure if it hit the far wall, but I vividly remember red sauce on the white tablecloth and a piece of half-chewed pasta stuck to my sister's face.

When was the last time you laughed uncontrollably? If you are like me, it has been far too long. When was the last time you had a good, long cry? Ditto. We have learned our childhood lessons all too well. *Repress your feelings. Control your reactions. Don't let anyone see what is going on inside. Protect yourself by hiding your heart and soul.* These unspoken lessons are taught not only by parents and teachers, but by the painful realities of life itself. The playground, the dance floor, and even the boardroom can be brutal classrooms for the lesson of emotional repression.

Many of us carry these lessons into worship to our own detriment. Consciously or unconsciously we ignore or squash various emotions as they arise, especially those deemed unacceptable by society or the church. However, the basis for this judgment is not so much what is biblical as what is comfortable. For many of us this is an attempt to maintain control. Since we cannot control which feelings might be evoked if we allow our worship to include emotional experiences, many of us tend to exclude the soul as an aspect of worship. No wonder we often feel bored in church and our services feel so flat and dispassionate!

As you come to worship how aware are you of your feelings? Part of our preparation for worship needs to include reflection on our emotional state and an explicit offering of those feelings, no matter what they are, to God. Remember, there are no "good" or "bad" feelings. Feeling "happy" in worship is no better or more pleasing to God than feeling "sad." What matters is what we do with our emotions. As we saw in the Psalms, biblical worshipers express both joy and sorrow, hope and despair to God. Loving God with all our soul means offering all our emotions no matter how we are feeling. When we repress or withhold our feelings in worship we are not giving ourselves fully to God. So prepare yourself for worship by doing an internal inventory; reflect on how you are really feeling, and offer those feelings to God.

> "Loving God with all our soul means offering all our emotions no matter how we are feeling."

As the service begins, engage yourself as fully as possible in what is happening. If you allow your mind to wander, you will not be able to feel the impact of the transforming truth that is being offered. If you are not singing the songs, the music is less likely to stir up an emotional response within you. Notice how worshiping with your heart, mind, and strength will help engage your soul. I find a direct relationship between how intentionally I am choosing to engage my mind and body in worship and the intensity of the emotions I experience. You can hear someone say the words "I love you" and feel nothing, but when those words are followed by a genuine hug, and you think about a time when that person showed kindness to you, the feelings of being loved will come with greater power.

Use your mind to connect the words you are singing or hearing with the needs you are feeling.

- If you are sad, notice words of comfort . . .
- If you are lonely, look for promises of God's presence . . .
- If you are afraid, focus on expressions of protection . . .
- If you are joyful, connect with words of celebration . . .
- If you are grateful, express it in phrases of thanks . . .

Use your imagination to open your soul to God. Picture the things you are singing about, imagine Jesus right there in front of you as you worship. If you are not feeling meaningful emotions in your worship, maybe you have not fully engaged your mind with your soul.

Use your body to help your soul experience the God you are worshiping. I find when I engage my hands while singing, the emotional impact of the song is greatly heightened. Part of this is because it engages my mind more fully with what I am doing. In Chapter 6 I described some ideas for intentionally engaging your body in worship. Notice the emotional impact these kinds of physical gestures can have:

- When I kneel or bow in worship, I feel a more profound sense of humility in God's presence.
- When I lift my hands while singing words of exaltation, I feel greater awe in God's infinite power.
- When I place my hands over my heart while singing words of thanks, I feel deeper gratitude toward God for all he has done for me.
- When I cup my hands in front of me, I sense more fully the precious gift of grace God pours out on me.

It is a simple fact that you feel different when your body takes on different postures. Standing feels different than sitting. Bowing feels different than clapping. When I clap my hands and move my feet to a musical celebration of God's goodness I feel greater joy than if I stand still. Physical worship can allow the Holy Spirit to move us into an emotional experience that goes beyond words. Paul points to this when he describes how the "Spirit intercedes with sighs too deep for words" (Romans 8:26). If you are not feeling moving emotions in your worship, maybe it is because you have not fully engaged your body with your soul.

The creative arts are a wonderful key God has given us to unlock the door to our soul and help us feel his presence. You have probably heard it said that music is the language of the soul. Let the artistic beauty of the music in your service stir up feelings you didn't know you had. Abraham Heschel said, "A work of art introduces us to emotions which we have never cherished before. Great works produce rather than satisfy needs by giving the world fresh cravings."[3]

If there are other creative expressions incorporated in your worship—a dance, a drama, a story, a scene from a film—open yourself to what God wants to do through them. When you feel unexpected emotions arising within you, resist the urge to repress or control them. Just offer those feelings to God along with your thoughts, physical acts, and choices. Ask the Holy Spirit to fill you and consciously yield control to him. If something stirs your soul with joy, smile. If something strikes you as funny, laugh. If something moves you deeply, cry. God will use your feelings to add intensity to the truth you are hearing, meaning to the things you are doing, and conviction to the decisions you are making.

Feeling Our Worship

Saul of Tarsus was a deeply intellectual person. As a Pharisee he knew more about God than most of us, and yet his life was profoundly out of sync with God's purpose. When he came face to face with Jesus on the road to Damascus, it was an experience so intense that his whole life was changed. Saul not only came to understand God had revealed himself in Jesus Christ, but he was filled with a passion to follow and serve Jesus no matter what the cost. Saul, better known to us as Paul, describes this shift from knowledge to commitment; "My speech and my proclamation were not with plausible words of wisdom, but with a demonstration of the Spirit and of power, so that your faith might rest not on human wisdom but on the power of God" (1 Corinthians 2:4-5). Through our emotions the Holy Spirit can powerfully connect what we *know* with what we *do* through what we *feel*.

As we learn to open ourselves to emotional experiences in worship we will come to a place where the Holy Spirit can connect *truths* in our mind with *commitments* in our heart through *feelings* in our soul. These emotional experiences will open us to the transforming power of the Spirit who will lead us into a life of loving God with all our heart, soul, mind, and strength. Experiential Worshipers are willing to take the risk of allowing their emotions to move them into more complete expressions of love for God.

FOR REFLECTION AND DISCUSSION

1. Is your worship more or less emotional than the worship described in the Psalms? What does that tell you about this aspect of your worship life?

2. Since Jesus was so free about expressing the whole range of his emotions, what do you think often keeps us from expressing our feelings more openly in worship?

3. Are there some emotions that are inappropriate for public worship? What about during our private times of worship?

4. What are the risks of expressing our emotions in worship? What are the benefits?

5. Read Luke 7:36-50. Is your worship more like Simon the Pharisee or the woman who anointed Jesus? What would help you worship more like this amazing woman?

Chapter 9

THE FEAST THAT NEVER ENDS!

FISH AND FIRE

Charcoal smoke mixed with the smell of sizzling fish as Peter chewed his bread and in amazement stared across the fire... at Jesus cooking his breakfast! His mind raced back over the incomprehensible events which had unfolded these past few days. His soul was wracked with shame for choices he had made. That terrible moment at the house of Caiaphas when the rooster crowed. And just last night he had begun to doubt the appearances they experienced back in Jerusalem. Maybe they had imagined him after all. Grieving minds can do strange things. It was so different before—Jesus was there all the time to show them the way. Peter just couldn't figure out what all of this meant and didn't know what to do next.

Seeking comfort in the familiar, they had gone home to the lake. Without even thinking about it, Peter pulled out their old boat and started rigging the nets. Thomas, Nathaniel, James, John, and a couple of the others joined him, but fishing only made things worse. Though they worked all night and hit all their old spots, not a single fish appeared in their nets. Then, just at daybreak, someone called to them from the shore, "Cast the net to the right side of the boat!"

Whoever this was obviously didn't know much about fishing. If a whole night netted them nothing, one more try when the prime feeding time was over certainly wouldn't accomplish anything. But an indiscernible memory began to stir in Peter and he cast out the net again. As they drew in the lines, the surface of the water started to churn, and then the rope started to burn their hands. Instinctively, everyone grabbed on and pulled with all their might, but they still couldn't land this incredible catch. Turned out it was 153 fish in one cast!

Only once before had something like that ever happened on this lake; the day Jesus called them to fish for people. Clearly this was him, risen from the dead and calling them anew. Peter remembered falling down in awe at Jesus' feet that day, blurting out "Go away from me, Lord, for I am a sinful man!" Peter thought, *How much has changed, and yet so little,* remembering his triple denial of Jesus back in Jerusalem, just as the Master had predicted.

Now they were gathered around the fire with Jesus and no one knew what to say. Peter kept staring, but whenever Jesus looked at him he would turn his eyes away. Finally Jesus broke the silence, asking Peter the piercing question, "Simon son of John, do you love me more than these?" A surge of regret welled up inside of Peter at these words. He knew his bold proclamations from the past meant nothing because he hadn't lived up to his own promises. "Yes, Lord; you know that I love you."

Jesus said to him, "Feed my lambs." Jesus asked the question again and when Peter repeated his answer, Jesus said, "Tend my sheep." When Jesus asked a third time, Peter finally understood Jesus was uncovering the shame of his three-fold denial. It hurt.

But the pain of this realization was like a surgeon excising a festering wound. Peter knew loving Jesus meant giving his whole life back to him without reservation, without condition, loving him with all of his heart, soul, mind, and strength. "Lord, you know everything; you know that I love you." Jesus said to him, "Feed my sheep."

Suddenly Peter realized what Jesus was doing. *He still wants me to feed his sheep! Me!* Peter finally understood Jesus wasn't punishing him for his three denials; he was forgiving him, restoring him, reinstating him as leader of the disciples! Wonder and relief flooded his soul as his heart swelled with a new passion to follow Jesus and serve him, no matter what the cost. Even if it meant dying, Peter knew that now he could never deny Jesus again. (Based on John 21:1-19)

No Ordinary Meal

There is a fire burning on the shores of our complacency. A meal is waiting for us beyond our resistance and shortsightedness. In spite of all our bravado and false promises, even after repeated denials, Jesus is preparing delights for us. He waits for us in the fog of our self-absorption. He watches us flail our nets in dark, unproductive waters. He calls to us across the sea and offers more than we can imagine; a feast where we will eat and finally be restored.

This is no ordinary meal. This is not the fast-food of our drive-through McChurches, bloating the stomach while rotting the soul. It is a feast born in sacrifice and suffering. It is the fruit of a love willing to give everything for the beloved. It is the rarest of delicacies: an omnipotent and holy God who freely chooses to give himself away completely.

> "This is no ordinary meal . . . It is the rarest of delicacies: an omnipotent and holy God who freely chooses to give himself away completely. It is the meal without which we will surely die."

It is the meal without which we will surely die.

The invitation to this meal is not ordinary either. It comes with no vacuous promise to feed our egos or satisfy our demands. It offers no quick fixes or superficial makeovers. It nurtures neither consumerist impulses nor self-addictions. It is a call to come and die, to give ourselves away, to become smaller so God might become bigger in us. It is an invitation in which we receive the Source of all we long for by giving up all we have held so tightly.

My son Bobby has always been a collector. When he was still a toddler he loved to go to the mall knowing he could slip away in the blink of an eye underneath the racks of clothing and merchandise to find seemingly limitless "treasures." He would reappear, his cherubic face flushed with joy and tiny fists overflowing with discarded price tags, pieces of broken hangers, and assorted other merchandising castoffs. To try and separate the treasure hunter from his treasure was as dangerous as entering a pirate's secret cave, so our established practice was to allow him whatever he could carry. One day we emerged from a department store into the mall and passed in front of an ice cream store. Unable to resist that tiny voice using the magic word "please," I immediately bought him a chocolate cone, but suddenly the dilemma became crystal clear to both of us. As I handed the cone to him he was torn with the decision: let go of half his "treasure" or miss out on the delicious chocolate ice cream!

We find ourselves facing a similar dilemma. Our heavenly Father freely offers the object of our deepest longings; a life lived in passionate love with the Giver of all good things. And yet we cling to our pride, position, possessions, reputation, comforts, pleasures, and above all, our sense of control. Will we finally let go and receive the gift offered to us? Or will we continue to clench in our fists the trinkets we have endued with such importance? Inevitably we want to add worship to our collection of baubles, twisting it into another means to our own ends. This is the fattening fodder of our sinful self-absorption, another marketable meal on the menu of our consumerist culture. But this is not the feast that Jesus offers.

As we have seen, Jesus calls us to love God with all we are, heart, soul, mind, and strength. This is an invitation to experience God in worship through our choices, our feelings, our understanding, and our actions. We may be tempted to think of worship primarily in terms of what we want, what we get, and how we feel, but first and foremost Experiential Worship is not about us. Peter was thinking of himself when he began to sink on the waters of Galilee, when he resisted Jesus' prediction of suffering and death, when he denied Jesus three times in the courtyard of the High Priest. This is why Jesus lovingly persisted in asking Peter, "Do you love me?" He kept asking until Peter was able to turn from his own sin and shame and receive the grace being offered so freely. He kept asking until Peter could look into Jesus' eyes and see him for who he is. He kept asking until Peter could look beyond himself and accept a call to serve others rather than live in slavery to his own agenda.

Paul helps us understand the divine trajectory of Experiential Worship when he describes true worship as "a living sacrifice, holy and acceptable to God" (Romans 12:1). Rather than offering sacrificial animals, in the grace of the crucified and risen Jesus we are now called to *die* to our sinful selves and *live* as an ongoing act of worship. Loving God means offering our thoughts in all we do, our emotions no matter how we feel, our whole body as an instrument of praise, every choice we make to glorify him. This kind of worship is not about us, it is about God. And yet paradoxically, when we finally get our eyes off ourselves and onto God, we begin to experience the fulfillment of all we have sought so long.

> "Loving God means offering our thoughts in all we do, our emotions no matter how we feel, our whole body as an instrument of praise, every choice we make to glorify him."

From Turkish Delight to Aslan's Table

In C. S. Lewis' masterpiece *The Lion, the Witch, and the Wardrobe*, upon entering the magical land of Narnia the boy Edmund is ensnared by the wicked White Witch when she offers him enchanted Turkish Delight, the manifestation of his perceived greatest desire. As Lewis describes it, "Each piece was sweet and light to the very center and Edmund had never tasted anything more delicious."[14] The only problem with this scrumptious treat is the more Edmund eats, the greater his longing for more becomes. Even worse, when deprived of more he becomes increasingly aware of just how sick it is making him feel. The Witch promises him unlimited Turkish Delight in exchange for his cooperation with her plan, which ultimately leads Edmund to betray the ones he loves the most and unwittingly enslaves him to everything he stands against.

Today we are constantly offered Turkish Delight. A hundred times a day we are told what will fulfill our deepest longings. Countless empty promises are made, none of which ultimately satisfy. No wonder we approach worship as a commodity to feed our self-serving appetites! How easily we can be enslaved to a mindset about worship ruled by our own familiarity, preferences, and convenience. How many churches are torn apart because we have insisted on a worship style that meets our own exacting demands? How many ministry leaders are attacked and demoralized because we have put our own desires above the greater good of the community and the greater mission of the church? But make no mistake, it is slavery when we make worship all about us. The evil one delights in an enslavement to self that infects even such a God-oriented act as worship. This is not the meal that Jesus offers; it is a deceptive enticement which causes us to deny everything we stand for and leaves us spiritually sick.

In *The Voyage of the Dawn Treader*, book five in Lewis' *Chronicles of Narnia*, Prince Caspian, Lucy, Edmond, Eustace, and their crew set sail on an adventure to discover the fate of the seven lost lords of Narnia. Their voyage brings them eventually to an island near the edge of the Narnian world where they discover Aslan's Table, set on a long stone pavement surrounded by carved pillars and silk-cushioned chairs. Standing in amazement they gawk at the meal set before them:

> "On the table itself there was set out such a banquet as had never been seen, not even when Peter the High King kept his courts at Cair Paravel. There were turkeys and geese and peacocks, there were boars' heads

and sides of venison, there were pies shaped like ships under full sail or like dragons and elephants, there were ice puddings and bright lobsters and gleaming salmon, there were nuts and grapes, pineapples and peaches, pomegranates and melons and tomatoes. There were flagons of gold and silver and curiously-wrought glass; and the smell of the fruit and the wine blew toward them like a promise of all happiness."[5]

Even more marvelous than the ingredients of this incredible meal at Alsan's Table was the fact it was miraculously renewed every day to offer an endless supply of perfectly fresh delicacies for all who would sit and enjoy it. When the travelers arrived on this scene they were surprised to find the three final Narnian lords of their quest, seated at the table and surrounded by all these delicacies, but deeply asleep and unable to eat them. Finally, when the travelers completed their voyage to the End of the World, the lords were awakened from their enchanted sleep and joined them in a feast at Aslan's Table like none they had ever tasted!

Many of us today are seated at Aslan's Table but have not yet joined in the feast. Maybe we have gorged ourselves on Turkish Delight and our self-addiction has cast us into a deep sleep. Maybe we have substituted outward forms and personal preferences for the true content of worship, a complete encounter with God himself. Maybe we are missing some critical ingredients which are keeping us from enjoying the meal set before us. Have you limited worship to a head trip or outward rituals or concrete choices or subjective feelings? Have you closed off a part of yourself and withheld something from your offering to

God? If so, you are missing out on the incredible banquet that is being served all around you!

Jesus comes and calls us out of our slumber: "People will come from east and west, from north and south, and will eat in the kingdom of God." "For those who want to save their life will lose it, and those who lose their life for my sake, and for the sake of the gospel, will save it . . . you shall love the Lord your God with all your heart, and with all your soul, and with all your mind, and with all your strength." (Luke 13:29; Mark 8:35; 12:30). Jesus announced the Good News of the Kingdom that alone has the power to break the spell we are under, the power of a God who loves us beyond our imagining, the power of a God who suffered and died for us and now lives inside us. No more Turkish Delight! No more slavery to self-worship! The time has come for us to heed Jesus' call, be filled with the gracious power of his Spirit, and awaken to the life for which God created us, a life lived in constant communion with him, a life of Experiential Worship.

IMAGINE EXPERIENTIAL WORSHIP

Imagine what this kind of worship-life is like, when every outside distraction and thought of self slips away and you are pouring your whole self out to God. You bow your entire body in a posture of stunned reverence, your mind reels with truths too huge to contain, your soul explodes with unbounded passion for the God of your salvation, and your heart bursts with a longing to follow Jesus and do his will. This is Experiential Worship! This is what we were made for.

Now imagine an entire church of people worshiping in this way, using their whole bodies as instruments of praise, intentionally engaging the word with their minds to understand more and more of who God really is. Enflamed by this truth, they pour out all their emotions with great passion as a sacred offering and translate this experience into deliberate decisions. This is a community engaged in Experiential Worship. I don't know about you, but that's a church I want to be part of!

Now imagine those people streaming out of that church into the world, demonstrating in their daily lives the very character of the God they worship. Giving themselves to God becomes the heartbeat of their very existence, as natural as breathing is to the body. Simple things like taking a hot shower or eating a good breakfast are so infused with feelings of gratitude that they become sacred moments of thanksgiving to God. Time spent in the word, images of the world around them, interaction with fellow travelers, and the meaning of daily events become means by which God speaks the truth to the minds of these 24/7 worshipers. The wonders of creation, from the tiniest cell to the most massive supernova, transform the entire cosmos into a sanctuary where awe empowers choices that glorify God by demonstrating his love to friends and strangers near and far. The outward physical actions of these Experiential Worshipers are increasingly in concert with the will of their heavenly Father and so step by step they enter more fully into the kingdom which Jesus promised to those who seek him.

Jesus invites you to join him on the voyage of a lifetime, an adventure that will lead you into a life you never imagined. The wind is blowing the fragrance of fruit and wine toward you like a promise of lasting joy and peace—can you smell it? This table is laden with a feast unlike any you have ever known—can you taste it? No longer do you have to wait for Thanksgiving or stale memories sealed in a jar: this feast is fresh every day, endlessly renewed, freely available.

It is precious because it cost God everything.

It is free because Jesus gave his life for us.

It is fulfilling because in it the Spirit gives himself to us.

It is life-giving because in giving ourselves completely to God we finally begin to truly live. You're seated at Jesus' table. Can you see him across from you? Awaken to this feast and give God all your heart, mind, soul, and strength; you will never be hungry again.

FOR REFLECTION AND DISCUSSION

1. What is the Turkish Delight in your life that has left you feeling empty and unfulfilled?

2. Have you been sleeping at Aslan's Table and missing out on some of the feast laid out for you? What will help you wake up and partake more fully?

3. What are the "treasures" you will need to let go of in order to receive the joy of more complete worship?

4. Have you experienced the paradox Jesus describes when you receive by giving yourself away? What does this mysterious dynamic teach us about the nature of true worship?

5. Read John 21:1-19. Imagine Jesus is asking you, "Do you love me?" What can you do to answer that question with more than just your words? How can your worship life help answer that question in the affirmative?

NOTES

1. Saint Augustine of Hippo, *Confessions*, X, 27.38 (New York: Penguin Books, 1961, 1985), p. 231.
2. Kathleen Norris, *The Cloister Walk* (New York: Riverhead Books, 1996), p. 346-347.
3. Bob Rognlien, *Experiential Worship: Encountering God with Heart, Soul, Mind, and Strength* (Colorado Springs, Colo.: NavPress, 2005). Also, The Experiential Worshiper Churchwide Campaign Kit. See www.experientialworship.com and below, pages 123-127, for more information.
4. Matt Redman, "Revelation and Response," *The Heart of Worship Files* (Ventura, Calif.: Regal, 2003), p. 13.
5. Martin Luther, "Dedication Sermon for the Church in Torgau, Luke 14:1-11, October 5, 1544," *Luther's Works*, CD-ROM edition (Minneapolis, Minn.: Fortress Press; 2001) vol. 51, p. 333.
6. Louie Giglio, *The Air I Breathe: Worship as a Way of Life* (Sisters, Ore.: Multnomah, 2003), p. 51.
7. Bob Rognlien, *Experiential Worship: Encountering God with Heart, Soul, Mind, and Strength* (Colorado Springs, Colo.: NavPress, 2005). Also, The Experiential Worshiper

Churchwide Campaign Kit. See www.experientialworship
.com and below, pages 123-127, for more information.

8. Foster, p. 158.

9. Dallas Willard, *Renovation of the Heart: Putting on the Character of Christ* (Colorado Springs, Colo.: NavPress, 2002), p. 159, emphasis mine.

10. Matt Redman, *The Unquenchable Worshiper* (Ventura, Calif.: Regal, 2001), p. 41.

11. Bob Rognlien, *Experiential Worship: Encountering God With Heart, Soul, Mind, and Strength* (Colorado Springs: NavPress, 2005). Also, *The Experiential Worshiper Churchwide Campaign Kit*. See www.experientialworship.com for more information.

12. Michael Card, *A Sacred Sorrow: Reaching Out to God in The Lost Language of Lament* (Coloroado Springs, Colo.: NavPress: 2005), p. 21, back cover.

13. As quoted in Ken Gire, *Windows of the Soul* (Grand Rapids, Mich.: Zondervan, 1996), p. 84.

14. C. S. Lewis, *The Lion, the Witch, and the Wardrobe* (New York: HarperCollins, 1950, 1994), p. 37.

15. C. S. Lewis, *The Voyage of the Dawn Treader* (New York: HarperCollins, 1952, 1994), p.192-193.

About the Author

Bob Rognlien's passion is to see people's lives changed through more complete, biblical experiences of God in worship. Having lived on both coasts of the United States, as well as in Europe, the Middle East, and the Far East, he has worshiped God in many different cultures and traditions. A graduate of Princeton Theological Seminary, Bob has also studied in Tacoma, Washington; Berkeley, California; Kent, England; Berlin, Germany; and Jerusalem. He has served churches in New Jersey and Jerusalem, as well as Northern and Southern California.

As Senior Pastor of Lutheran Church of the Good Shepherd, Bob is privileged to be part of a life-changing community that is exploring new ways to worship God with heart, soul, mind, and strength. He is a sought-after national conference speaker and has engaged thousands of leaders on innovative worship and preaching around the world. Bob is available to provide inspiring and insightful keynote presentations introducing a more complete kind of worship and developing these kinds of experiences in your community.

Bob's greatest joy is sharing life with his wife Pam and his sons Bobby and Luke. He makes his home with them in Torrance, California where he loves to surf, ski, sail, paddle, backpack, cook, read, and go to the movies. Contact Bob at bob@experientialworship.com and join the collaborative community of experiential worshipers by signing up for the free newsletter at www.experientialworship.com.

INTRODUCE EXPERIENTIAL WORSHIP
TO YOUR WHOLE CHURCH!
"The Experiential Worshiper Churchwide Campaign Kit"

Here's everything your church needs to put on a six-week Experiential Worship series called "The Whole Enchilada," along with resources for weekly small groups and daily readings for every member.

Includes:

- CD-ROM with worship themes, worship orders, PowerPoint slides with graphics, sermon outlines, creative ideas, and implementation guide.

- Small Group DVD with six creative teaching segments by Bob Rognlien to introduce each of the six small group sessions, plus a bonus training segment for small group leaders. Includes small group leader's guide.

- A copy of the original book, *Experiential Worship: Encountering God with Heart, Soul, Mind, and Strength* for the leaders of your church.

- A copy of this book, *The Experiential Worshiper: Giving Yourself More Completely to God*, which will provide daily readings for the members of your church.

> When you purchase the Churchwide Campaign Kit, it qualifies your church for 50% bulk discounts on copies of The Experiential Worshiper and the Small Group DVD.

Order now at www.experientialworship.com!